Something About Knowing God

Something About Knowing God

Seeing Through His Eyes from Brokenness to Wholeness

VERA L. SMITH

Foreword by Carol Breiling

RESOURCE *Publications* · Eugene, Oregon

SOMETHING ABOUT KNOWING GOD
Seeing Through His Eyes from Brokenness to Wholeness

Copyright © 2025 Vera L. Smith. All rights reserved. Except for brief quotations in critical publications or reviews, no part of this book may be reproduced in any manner without prior written permission from the publisher. Write: Permissions, Wipf and Stock Publishers, 199 W. 8th Ave., Suite 3, Eugene, OR 97401.

Resource Publications
An Imprint of Wipf and Stock Publishers
199 W. 8th Ave., Suite 3
Eugene, OR 97401

www.wipfandstock.com

PAPERBACK ISBN: 979-8-3852-6144-4
HARDCOVER ISBN: 979-8-3852-6145-1
EBOOK ISBN: 979-8-3852-6146-8

VERSION NUMBER 120125

Scripture marked (NKJV) taken from the New King James Version®. Copyright © 1982 by Thomas Nelson. Used by permission. All rights reserved.

Scripture marked (NASB) taken from the New American Standard Bible®, Copyright © 1960, 1971, 1977, 1995, 2020 by The Lockman Foundation. All rights reserved.

Scripture quotations marked (AMP) taken from the Amplified® Bible (AMP), Copyright © 2015 by The Lockman Foundation. Used by permission. lockman.org.

Scripture quotations marked (AMPC) taken from the Amplified® Bible (AMPC), Copyright © 1954, 1958, 1962, 1964, 1965, 1987 by The Lockman Foundation Used by permission. lockman.org.

Scripture quotations marked (NIV) taked from THE HOLY BIBLE, NEW INTERNATIONAL VERSION®, NIV® Copyright © 1973, 1978, 1984, 2011 by Biblica, Inc.® Used by permission. All rights reserved worldwide.

Scripture quotations marked (NLT) taked from the *Holy Bible*, New Living Translation, copyright © 1996, 2004, 2015 by Tyndale House Foundation. Used by permission of Tyndale House Publishers, Inc., Carol Stream, Illinois 60188. All rights reserved.

A second book dedicated in memory of my beloved mother who was born as Ruth Berry. Although your time in my life was much too brief, the memories of you remain as a storeroom of precious treasures. In this book, I share your unimaginable and painful story which I believe will speak to the heart of those who have experienced unexpected and uninvited struggles in life. Father God, I thank You again for molding with Your hands this precious jewel of a gift whom I miss deeply.

Beyond my dedication to my beloved mother, I dedicate this book back to God.

I will give thanks to the Lord with all my heart; I will tell of all Thy wonders.

—Psalm 9:1

O Lord, you have searched me [thoroughly] and have known me. 2. You know when I sit down and when I rise up [my entire life, everything I do]; You understand my thought from afar. 3. You scrutinize my path and my lying down, and You are intimately acquainted with all my ways.

—Psalm 139:1–3

(Amplified Bible/AMP. The Lockman Foundation.)

Contents

Foreword by Carol Breiling | ix

Preface | xi

Acknowledgements | xv

Introduction | xix

Author's Story: Through the Eyes of A Child | xxiii

Looking Back | xxvi

Chapter 1: Growing Pains | 1
    Never Meant to Stay Broken | 1
    Pulling My Little Red Wagon | 7
    Seeing Through His Eyes | 14
    Yet Will I Hope in Him | 18
    My God, My Healer | 21
    In The Midst of it All | 26
    No Fear? | 32

Chapter 2: An Uphill Climb | 37
    God Brought Us Through | 37
    Dressing In The Full Armor of God | 44
    From Shame to Glory! | 49
    God Has Something Better | 51
    Building A New Foundation | 55
    Dancing in The Rain | 60
    It's Time to Lay it All Down | 63

Chapter 3: Timely Reflections | 69
    The Place Where We Are | 69
    God is Intentional | 74
    Learning To be Happy in Your Storm | 78
    Power in the Name | 83
    No Greater Love | 85
    Mama | 89
    It's Just God's Way | 90
    Know Who You Are | 94
    Where Do We Go From Here? | 98

Revelation 3:20–22 | 105

Also by Vera L. Smith | 106

Author's Biography | 107

Bibliography | 111

Index | 113

Foreword

In 2010, I was blessed to have met Vera Smith at an Employment Placement Workshop for former military members. It was also during a season in my life where I was being hammered with my own spiritual warfare. I faced challenges on my professional path as a new mental health clinician. I found myself trying to balance my professional life with connections to friend groups that primarily consisted of other individuals who were also weighed down by emotional stressors. Vera stepped into my life as a mentor at just the right time. Through her wisdom, I learned a sense of freedom comes not only from setting healthier boundaries with others, but more profoundly from the grace and freedom I gained from the difficult task of self-forgiveness that was needed before I could even apply such boundaries with others. Vera helped me to tune-out the self-doubt and negative thoughts that began to grip me as a new clinician. The basic lessons she mentored me on became a turning point for me, allowing me to walk my journey in peace and strength, rather than sheer mental exhaustion and confusion. I was way too early in my career to be experiencing burn-out.
Over the years, and now a psychologist, I have walked with many others who carry stories of emotional pain and longing for healing. Too often, individuals believe their wounds disqualify them from wholeness. Yet, Vera's testimony stands as a powerful witness that the opposite is true—our struggles, when surrendered to God, become the very soil where resilience, purpose, and divine intimacy take root. In her book, she shows all of us that God does not waste our tears, our trials, or our questions.

That is the gift Vera offers readers in "Something About Knowing God". Not only do all of the stories create her testimony – they are being used as a guiding light for others who seek wholeness in the midst of brokenness. Vera's words remind us that God meets us in our struggles and gently reshapes them into strength, purpose, and renewal. The stories she

Foreword

tells are sacred offerings born out of lived experience—experiences marked by loss, perseverance, faith, and ultimately, transformation. Just as it was for me personally.

The raw honesty with which Vera recounts her journey, from the eyes of a child witnessing unthinkable tragedy to the heart of a woman who has walked through many storms with steadfast trust, Vera reminds all of us that our periods of brokenness does not have to define us. A statement I still use almost every day in my practice when I tell my clients, "Our past does not have to define our future". Vera demonstrates perseverance she models throughout this book, especially when she makes soft, but powerful statements such as, "In God's hands, our broken places can actually make us vessels for His glory". How forgiving and insightful is that statement? It's just one of many testimonies she shared that you can draw peace and comfort from as well, just turn the pages and read on.

"Something About Knowing God" is not only Vera's story; it is also an invitation. An invitation to the reader to see through God's eyes, to find hope in the valleys, and to embrace the truth that in every storm, there is a seed of renewal within it. Vera's reflections are both practical and deeply spiritual, weaving scripture and poetry in a way that speaks to the intellect, the heart, and the soul.

Whether you are emerging from a storm, caught in its fury, or sensing one approaching you out there on the horizon, you will find healing, comfort and courage throughout the pages. Vera's words carry the weight of lived faith and the lightness of His divine grace.

It is with great honor that I commend "Something About Knowing God" to you. May it be a companion in your journey, a soft pillow for your suffering to land on, and a reminder that the God who knows us most intimately also loves us most completely. May your troubles be nothing more than a snapshot in time and never your whole story. What will He unfold in you through your next struggle?

— Dr. Carol Breiling, PsyD

Preface

IN UNDERSTANDING SOMETHING ABOUT knowing God three things come to mind—things I did not know before, a reminder of things I had forgotten, and learning how to shape things we all have in common while understanding that none of us have it all. The real-life stories included in this book are meshed with glimpses and reminders of relevant biblical history and Scripture all to inspire, impact, and to speak to life's personal struggles and conditions that arise today, as well as to bring closure where closure is needed.

Over 40 years ago my story began in my thirst to know God more intimately. One day while reading the Bible, I felt deeply bothered by some of the behaviors of God's people in the Old Testament. In fact, I murmured to myself about their behaviors when suddenly, I perceived that God was speaking to me about some of my own behaviors. Awestruck, and feeling intense conviction and remorse, I repented. But at the same time, there was something else I sensed taking place. I sensed God was also giving me the spiritual name of Judah. Never had heard of anything like this before and so for about three days, I kept what I believed had occurred to myself. Finally after working up the courage to share with a close friend, I was amazed to learn that a year earlier, she also had a similar experience with God giving her a spiritual name. Over the next few years, while God was still developing my awareness to recognizing His voice, whenever I would ask Him a question about matters concerning my personal life, He would lead me to a specific passage in the Bible that referenced the tribe of Judah. Again, I would sense that God was talking to me about myself. I came to the place of not only recognizing God's voice, but I grew to understand God is not limited to who we think He is. God is who He reveals Himself to be. Giving me a spiritual name was the second epochal moment I remember experiencing something quite different and unexpected with God. The first epochal moment is mentioned in the next part of this book. Surprisingly to me, while thinking it was a bit peculiar about God assigning to me a spiritual name, I can look back to remember this same phenomena took place numerous times in the Bible as recalled a little further on in this book.

Arriving at a place of knowing something more about knowing who God is, my road has been one of kneeling in His presence and oftentimes questioning His silence while weathering a barrage of stormy seasons. Time spent often walking in solitude with God has given me inspiring life stories that cut through the quagmire of doubt and despair and longing for answers only for God to reveal His presence in small intimate details often overlooked. My time spent alone with God as disclosed on the pages of this book makes known to the reader that in every season of life, God is forging instruments of strength and endurance out of fiery furnace experiences that enable us to come out changed on the other side to reveal His glory in our testimonies and life stories. Changed to help heal the brokenhearted. Changed to uplift the spirit of those around us who need to hear an encouraging word that helps them prepare beforehand for their appointed destiny. Our pain and our struggles are not wasted as we cry out to God because He hears our cries, and He answers. Something that I had forgotten written many years ago in my Bible above the Scripture Zechariah 13:9 is the note, "He refines us so that the Refiner is able to see His image." As we journey forward, God makes us wise in not only recognizing destructive spirits before we let them in, but He refines us so that we feel peace in solitude and come to recognize that our worth is not based on a path of walking with many. We choose quality over quantity. From handwritten notes that uncover much of my journey with God, this book captures something about knowing God while walking in intimate fellowship with Him as He built a life story revealing this truth—God girds our loins with humility, insight, and compassion to encourage others to place their hope in Him. He clothes us with divine wisdom and understanding to perceive that our own self-worth and quiet strength are bathed solely in Him to help strengthen and heal others. Solitude can be a calling.

A little bit about how the title of this book came about. About seven years ago while talking with someone whom I relished as a friend, I was trying to come up with a working title and I just so happened to say to her, "It needs to be something about knowing God." With excitement in her voice, she exclaimed, "That's it! That's it, Vera!" "What's it?!" I asked in bewilderment. "Something About Knowing God! That's the title of the book!"

Preface

A few years had passed by, but over the course of this last year, my heart was stirred to begin working on and completing this book. I should say working towards completing *His* book because our life stories are written to reveal something about knowing God. This is my fifth book—another book to lift up His great name.

When it came to the Preface, one night a peculiar thing happened. Suddenly awakened out of a sound sleep, I sensed God was speaking to me about the Preface to this book. After listening, I turned my head to see what time it was. Three fifty-five a.m. was displayed by the small green digital figures on my nightstand clock, but actually it was 3:45 because my clock is set 10 minutes ahead of time. The first thought that came to mind was *Uh, I am so sleepy, too sleepy to get up*. But I did get up because I have come to know something about knowing God that when He speaks He is speaking for a reason, and we are to move at this precise moment.

Back to my journey in writing this book. As I walked alone with God, He opened my eyes to recognize what matters most to me is something I believe matters most to Him—those struggling to make it in life who need to know His Name. Those who may not realize their intrinsic value and are not able to believe that living on the inside of them is a sleeping and undisturbed wealth of purpose and talent just waiting to be set free. In the midst of it all, God always reserves a word where iron sharpens iron as illustrated in my transparent real-life stories that come alongside both women and men alike. I believe God delivers a timely word in the right season as we follow in the steps of our Lord and Savior Jesus Christ while going about our Father's business.

> Oh, the depth of the riches both of the wisdom and knowledge of God! How unsearchable are His judgements, and unfathomable His ways! 34. For who has known the mind of the Lord, or who became His counselor? (Romans 11:33–34) (NASB95)

Acknowledgements

ANOTHER SOLO PROJECT COMPLETED during my time alone with God. So again, I thank God profusely for guiding me through writing another book. I acknowledge God first because without Him, I would not have known how to write the encouraging life stories as seen through the eyes of this earthen vessel. From where I began in life, who would have known God would take what was once broken and mold someone useful for His glory. Heavenly Father, I thank You for the voice You have given me and portions of Your wisdom You have poured into me to help liberate and to bring hope to those You love. I give honor, praise, and thanks to Your Great Name. You are my life story. You are my testimony.

To my precious and beautiful mother Ruth Berry. Although it has been over 60 years since you went home to be with our Lord, your genuine warmth and caring spirit will always be remembered not only by me, but also by those who came to know you. I still recall seeing the neighborhood kids gathering around our front porch whenever you would bake something sweet. They wanted it too. In my spirit, I can envision you with our heavenly Father where all is well. Though I miss you terribly, I know you are in a better place.

To my sons, Bryon, and Bobby. Truly this has been a journey walking with you while I walk with the Lord. In your growing up years, God had me teach you many things about the Bible and about His own character, His power, His love, and many of His godly principles for living life. As my struggles continued throughout your childhood years, I silently wrote about my life experiences that flowed with turbulent rising tides and calming low currents. I pray the journey God led me to write on the pages of this book and on the pages of other inspired books along with memories of my presence in your life will resonate throughout your life journey. Most importantly, I pray that God's presence and all He has led me to share with you

Acknowledgements

about who He is and the knowledge you have since gained about Him will resonate even more on the pages of your life story. I am thankful for our reading and prayer time together during your formative years as you listened intently, especially the time when we clapped our hands and praised God while circling our old coffee table seven times to knock down whatever was standing in the way of our future home. I followed the example in the Bible, and you witnessed God moving on behalf of your mama's guided prayers. I am reminded children are a gift from God and by leading you to Him, I've given you the best that I have.

To my grandson Victor for your unfailing love. You've always been there no matter how rough it got. Never leaving. And for this, I am truly thankful. I've seen in your life you have the love the Bible speaks about when it declares there is a friend who sticks closer than a brother. Your love runs deep, grandson, and I am thankful God gave you to me as a grandchild. I am thankful too that I could sit down with you from the time you were a little boy and even to now as a young adult to talk to you about my greatest friend—our Lord and Savior, and you still listen.

To my sister friend Neda. Oh, how you are missed my friend who many years ago saw something greater in me than I saw in myself. Write a book, write a book, write a book you would say, and I have. I pray for God's peaceful deliverance over the heartfelt challenge that unexpectedly came to erode your life. So thankful He gave me a sister friend like you.

To my close friend Elanda. I want you to know your encouraging texts about my first book still touches my heart in a special way. Only God could have allowed our friendship to survive distance and time. Elanda, I thank you for always letting me know just how special my first book written over 20 years ago continues to speak volumes to your heart today, a reminder that words are timeless.

To those whom I've met and have shared a kindred spirit and like compassion in many ways, I am thankful God allowed our paths to cross. You know who you are and you will always remain in my deepest thoughts.

I don't want to miss acknowledging those who read this book. May you glean insight from both tragedies and triumphs experienced on my journey with God spread across the fabric of my life that captures something about knowing God. May all God has led me to write be a blessing to you and to those you share my journey with.

From eyes that God opened while writing my previous book, *From My Heart To His Heart*, I now dedicate this book to my heavenly Father.

Acknowledgements

I Chronicles 29:13. "Now therefore, our God, we thank You and praise Your glorious name." (NKJV)

Introduction

"Victory is God's will for the life of a believer."[1] A profound truth illustrated throughout the Bible. But we don't triumph without suffering. We all must deal with challenges as we obtain and retain the victory that is ours as believers in Christ Jesus. From my growing up years, I would not have grasped this truth. And nor would I have known it prior to life experiences that led me to understand we can be intimately acquainted with God, deeply desiring to please Him yet we can still miss Him big time in certain areas of our lives. We can be 97% on target while the remaining and dangling 3% God is still working on while we grow in our intimacy with Him throughout our life's journey on the earth as we know it to be today. Sometimes I believe our understanding of God is just too limited so we miss the mark not because of anything that has to do with unrepented sin, but because the view we hold of God is just too small.

It's like the time about 40 years ago when I needed to take a typing test for a job I really wanted. I dreaded taking a timed test because of the mounting pressure inside me which caused me to make more than a dozen typing errors. One night while sharing with a close friend the fear I felt over having to take another timed typing test, unbeknownst to me after we prayed and ended our phone call, she went to God on my behalf with her own private prayer. Sad to say, even if I had known about the words she voiced in her petition to God on my behalf most likely it would not have changed my response to something I heard later that night. For the first time in my life in the wee hours of the morning, I heard Someone call out my name, only I didn't know who it was. Although I had been an avid student of the Bible, I had left God on the pages. I had reserved His voice only for those who lived during biblical times and I can tell you on the following

---

1. In Touch Ministries Daily Devotion (online). Inspired by The Teachings of Charles F. Stanley. "Overcoming Failure." November 19, 2024.

Introduction

day, I lived the aftermath of my disbelief and foolishness. This was the first epochal moment I experienced with God which full story is revealed in a previous book *When God Spoke To Me, He Said* . . .

Although I believe the Bible is God's love letter to the church, I also believe His love includes suffering. I see this manifested throughout the pages of the Bible as well as in my own life story. I see it when I listen to the testimonies and stories of others who answered the call of God. The matter of suffering as it relates to God's call upon a life reminds me of something I recently heard—"God takes His strongest servants through the hardest battles."[2]

Through painful life experiences of betrayal, job loss, seasons of suffering lack, being excluded from close-knit family circles, and experiencing unforeseen and difficult places which are candidly unveiled on the pages of this book, when peering through a spiritual lens, I see God was building trust and dependance solely upon Him to awaken and to inspire real-life stories that tell something about knowing God in ways only He can reveal.

Between the covers of this book, readers can learn valuable principles that help guide in understanding attributes of God they may not have realized when coping with unexpected life challenging struggles. Readers can arrive at recognizing unhealthy social attachments and when to leave someone in their past. Readers can learn to better identify and become keenly aware of the still small voice of God and ways to recover from the stigma of a past doused in regret and shame. I believe readers can also arrive at better understanding purpose and the power of prayer while learning relevant biblical history and Scriptures that resonant with life lived today. While growing to recognize God's presence in small intimate details, the readers are drawn closer to the heart of the God of the Bible. Readers can also enjoy treasurable moments of triumph and trusting God while struggling to understand His will. Readers can enjoy heartfelt moments of rejuvenating hope and moments of laughter that lessen the dregs left behind stinging life lessons and unexpected encounters. Overall, readers can sharpen their skills in coping successfully with life issues when eyes become opened to understanding that life lessons and unexpected storms can reveal far greater significance and insight than we first thought. Sometimes storms come to clear away old faulty ways of doing things. It's like what happened to me the other day.

---

2. Denzel Washington. Quote. YouTube online reel. September 29, 2024.

Introduction

As I walked through the auto service door at a Wal-Mart shopping center, the door hinges squeaked something awful. So when the cashier appeared, I mentioned to her that the door really needed oiling. But do you know what she said to me? "No it doesn't." Instantly, I thought to myself, *Can't she hear how loud the noise is from that door?* The next words she spoke to me took me to a new level in my spiritual understanding when she stated, "*That* door is my alarm system late at night to let me know when someone is coming so I won't be taken by surprise." I applied what I heard her say in a spiritual context because God's word is just like the picture she painted—no surface stuff. His word is packed with meaning so deep only He can reveal the fullness of its true value and intent so it's best to pay attention.

This book is filled with encouraging real-life stories filled with hope captured over years of walking in intimacy with God that disclose insight in learning something more about knowing God. As you read the life-stories in this book, I believe you will see that any feelings of regret and shame can become lessen upon realizing that what you've learned, although painful, wasn't wasted because it has armed you will spiritual tools to make guided decisions to safeguard your future and provide you with a renewed sense of self-worth. Pain, I discovered, is not without purpose. As wisely addressed by the late Doctor Myles Monroe, "Pain is the price of growth," and "Pain teaches what comfort never could."[3]

As evidenced today, the disorderly human behaviors we see or learn about reveal a desperate need for many to know something more about the heart of God in order to be set free in spirit and in truth. The behaviors seen today reveal a need for the spiritual blind to be infused with God's word of truth to walk humbly before Him which always makes a difference in guiding the actions we take.

As God spoke to the heart of His people long ago including a few of those who did not know His name, He continues to instill life-giving principles and hope to the hearts of earthen vessels appointed as instruments of change today. While God uses His people to He reveal His glory, we discover He hasn't lost His voice while we keep ours. So whether God uses human messengers, His written Word, His creation or His own still small voice or any other means He chooses to speak His word of truth through, the message is still His. Enjoy this book which is infused with words of

---

3. Dr. Myles Munroe YouTube online reel. Why God's Strongest Women Face the Hardest Battles. March 28, 2025.

Introduction

hope that encourages embracing self-worth while revealing the presence of God in our own life stories!

> Proverbs 3:5–6. "Trust in the Lord with all your heart and do not lean on your own understanding; 6. in all your ways acknowledge Him, and He will make your paths straight." (NASB95)

Author's Story
Through the Eyes of A Child

A PART OF THE story you are about to read was written many years ago to someone named Collis, a person I no longer remember. It would take me more than a few moments to figure out where I filed away the original notes written to him, so I retyped what I was able to find. I would surely like to know where I placed all my handwritten pages written to Collis about what matters most to me because I feel certain there is more to my story. Quoting from Page Two of the notes I wrote to Collis:

"What matters most to me are those struggling to make it in life. Those who do not understand buried deep inside may be a sleeping and undisturbed wealth of talent and inspiration just waiting to be set free. What matters most to me are the many people who need to hear encouraging and liberating words to aid in unlocking the door to birth their God-given dreams."

Precious words written in the Book of James remind us, "Every good thing given and every perfect gift is from above . . .."[1] All of our talents and giftings are God-given so I believe we all have encouraging and freeing God-inspired life stories and testimonies to tell. Now a little bit about my background.

I grew up not understanding my true value. Not understanding how God saw me as a person He loved. I grew up as a young person not understanding the life enduring benefits that result from making wise decisions which safeguard our present and our future. I grew up not understanding the importance of not transferring one's values to someone who hasn't earned them. Not understanding the unction of the Holy Spirit is meant to be heeded at all times because He is leading us into all truth. Thank God for

---

1. James Chapter 1, Verse 17. (NASB95)

Author's Story

opening eyes to understand that although we may not be able to erase our past, we can agree with God to write a bright future.

I was raised by my mother's murderer. Shortly after my eighth birthday and two days before the 4th of July, while outside playing, two of my siblings and I heard what we thought were firecracker sounds. I remember hearing a delay between the popping sounds so we continued on playing. But then we heard the popping sounds again and they seemed to be coming from our apartment so we ran across our backyard and flung open the screen door and the first thing we saw was our father standing outside our parents' bedroom door holding a gun in his hand. What we thought were firecracker sounds turned out to be gunshots fired into our mother's chest which silenced her life and the life of her unborn child. On this tragic day, through the eyes of a child, I watched my young pregnant mother bleeding from the chest as she lay dying from gunshot wounds. I might mention, during this time in my life, one mate killing another was an uncommon occurrence so I never talked about it. Although our dad was tried in the court system, the county determined that our dad and not the county nor would our Aunt Lettie provide for most of his 12 children who still lived at home. So after about five months of serving jail time, our dad came home again.

Life changed for us the day our mother died, and it changed again when our dad came home. Two of my oldest sisters who I grew up with were too afraid to stay in the same house with dad, so they left without us. Eventually, we moved out of that apartment, but over the years I learned three other people were also murdered inside the same apartment. This tells me a murdering spirit was still lingering there. Without any outside help or counseling, I grew up with flashbacks of seeing my mother die that day. Flashbacks of seeing her body propped up on the floor at the end of their bed. For years following this incident, I grew up unprepared to meet life's trials. As I grew older, I remained silent about this part of my life because how do you tell someone that you were raised by the person who took your mother's life?

But despite the stigma associated with this part of my life's journey and the setbacks met along the way while raising my two young sons as a single parent, today by the grace of God, I have been blessed to accomplish a few things mentioned on the back cover. My youngest son, a Stanford graduate, reminded me four years after initially writing the Author's Story that I had purchased a home, separately helped him and his brother in some way purchase a home, passed California's real estate exam on my first attempt

Author's Story

which opened the door to a new career. At the same time, God blessed me to publish my first inspired book while I pursued motivational speaking engagements within the local church.

God has brought me a long ways since my growing up years of living in the projects of a small, impoverished section of a Midwest community so today I reach back to help others see they too can rise from the depths of despair from a past riddled by painful memories. It is these people who need help to rise from years of shame and painful memories that mean the most to me. It is also those who desire to understand something more about knowing God. Although written over 40 years ago, I believe you can relate to my inspired poem about my growing up years written on the following page.

> 2 Corinthians 5:17. "Therefore if anyone is in Christ, he is a new creature; the old things passed away; behold new things have come." (NASB95).
>
> Revelation 1:17. "... and God will wipe away *every tear* from their eyes." (NASB95; emphasis mine).

Looking Back

Looking back through my eyes now,
   a little girl do I see,
who never was the little girl God intended her to be.
Looking back, I see many things that I'm not proud of.
Many things happened that weren't born out of love.

Dad was hard—no model of passion, nor patience nor love,
and now my mother rests in heaven above.
Many things happened that I'm not proud of.
Many things happened that weren't born out of love.

Cooking and ironing and washing and tending, too much too early.
Should have been playing jump rope, hopscotch, and leapfrog with my girlfriend Shirley.
A thousand times over I wished this was not my fate.
You are the reason you lost your mate.
Many things happened that I'm not proud of.
Many things happened that weren't born out of love.

Iron his clothes, fix his lunch, keep the house.
Did it make me stronger?
Being a kid should have lasted much longer.
Growing up fast, growing up not knowing
just what all of this was supposed to be showing.
Life was cruel, life was tough.
My dear brother left home in a huff.
Many things happened that I'm not proud of.
Many things happened that weren't born out of love.

No frills, no ruffles, not cherished, not protected.
No wonder many left home misdirected.
Shed tears, battle cries and wounds of war
did not prepare me for what was in store.

Author's Story

Unprepared to meet life's trials,
so often the enemy wore a face with a smile.
Many things happened that I'm not proud of.
Many things happened that weren't born out of love.

But my heavenly Father has put all things in their place.
Has prepared me now to run this race.
Cherished and protected, safeguarded, and directed.
Looking back now do I see,
the woman God has made that girl to be!

Vera L. Smith, Poet/Author

Chapter 1

Growing Pains

Never Meant to Stay Broken

WE DON'T ALWAYS LOOK like what we've been through because God takes what was once broken and makes it whole again. The once crooked and leaning places now stand upright in spirit and in truth as we follow His path which allows divine principles to operate in the core of our lives. What was once used and abused can be transformed into one of God's greatest instruments for change. In the hands of God, emotional exhaustion, seasons of isolation, the pain of disappointment and betrayal and other disruptions in life can all turn to yield seasoned fruit. Seasoned fruit packed with knowledge and wisdom and understanding needed to protect our inner peace and emotional energy as we keep in the forefront of our minds and heart the need to walk upright before the Lord our God. Christ came to set us free because God never meant for us to stay broken. God wants to make the broken places in your life whole.

Most people God uses to encourage others have been hurt or even devastated at some point in their life. An apt reminder taken from one of my previous books is to recognize many of those in the Bible who experienced brokenness were transformed and they changed the atmosphere and outcomes around them. Quoted by Khalil Gibran, "Out of suffering have emerged the strongest souls; the most massive characters are seared with scars."[1] From suffering, I have learned we not only experience some of the

---

1. The Epoch Times (online), 11/16/23.

pain Christ experienced, but we also develop a heart to hear others' pain. Maybe this is a reason why some people don't recognize your heartache.

For instance, have you ever wanted a loved one to understand your hurt about a life event but instead they condemn you? From firsthand experience, I know how it feels. You're already aching on the inside, and they come right along to knock you to the ground or at least try to. Contrary to this behavior, the Word of God instructs us to uplift the brokenhearted. To speak life to those around us. To speak words that edify but this won't happen if you don't come alongside the one suffering to offer words of hope and comfort.

In our Christlike service to others, First Peter 4:11 explains, "Whoever speaks, let him speak, as it were, the utterances of God."[2] Now where did those life draining words spoken to you come from? Words with the intent to tear down and not to build up. Words spoken not filtered through the Holy Spirit falling from lips that reveal a heart is far from God. Some people you thought were there for you do not even know His name. As local Pastor Colwell discernably questioned, "When you speak evil to a person who God has His eyes on, do you know what you are doing?"[3] Think carefully about what he said here because we should really consider the words that fall from our lips when we address those whom God loves. And this includes everybody, especially those close to God's own heart which brings to mind several places in the Bible where God has revealed His heart when it comes to how His chosen servants are spoken to.[4] I believe what God revealed about His heart long ago concerning His chosen people still resonates today. The best thing I have learned to do with ill-spoken and unfiltered words is to pray and give this person over to God. And also to stop accepting and allowing behaviors I don't deserve.

For those with a tender heart who love God and have been harmed by someone's uncaring behaviors or unfiltered words for you it is to understand Satan chases after the one who chases after God. So this may be your story. The enemy sees hidden treasure in you that you may not have seen in yourself. The enemy doesn't want anyone chosen by God to know who they truly are in Christ Jesus and to become aware of their true value. Even those with a tender heart who do not know the Lord the enemy will work arduously to keep them living blindly in order to sabotage or prevent a person

---

2. NASB95.
3. Taken from in-house sermon, 9/11/24.
4. Genesis 31:29, Numbers 12:8.

from choosing a relationship with God. The Word of God makes known to us we are created in His image which makes us intrinsically valuable. His word declares that we are fearfully and wonderfully made and we are the apple of His eye so it is never the words someone projects at you that are true about you when their own behavior does not reflect godly character. I think sometimes we forget the way we relate to others always reveals how we relate to God. The two are not separate. Am I ever thankful I know who I am in Him, and God wants you to know this too.

Any measure of wisdom God has given to me was not attained as a result of my upbringing. Nor did it come from time spent around those who I've come to realize were disjointed from walking out the genuine love of God. But God triumphed over every form of evil meant to keep me from rising. He broke chains from years of feeling crushed in spirit and from working on jobs where I became a target. You learn when you stand apart from the crowd people will see you as different, and it can become their relentless goal to make life hard for you. Yet God continued to work through me to help others at times when my own life was broken. He had deposited in me invaluable life principles to help bring others forward from places I had been. He kept me through the process of realizing the places that should have been safe circles of love only to find they were not safe at all. God kept me writing and growing in discernment and in my dependence upon Him because He never meant for any of us to stay broken. Sometimes God will isolate you *not* because of failure but because He is preparing and protecting you as you journey towards your destiny. Your life's purpose is not always understood by those closest to you while you are forming healthy boundaries which reflect wisdom, not the building of walls as they may see it. You may have been chosen to walk alone with God not out of stubbornness of heart but because you have been called by God for a divine mission for a time or season that He chooses. I have discovered that walking alone with God teaches resilience to stand alone, though every now and then He will send someone across your path for a season or a reason. I've also seen many times while walking alone with God, you don't even know where the help you need will come from. In these uncertain times, God has shown me that our dependence is to remain solely upon Him. When He chooses to use someone as His hands and feet, no matter whose hand He uses, it is still His hand that signs the bill. God *is* the reason we live and move and have our being.[5]

---

5. Acts 17:28 (NKJV).

If your life appears to be in shambles, know that your present state will not remain the way you see it now because over time, God shifts things for the best in your life just as He has done for me. I am not where I used to be. If you happen to be in a place of desiring to use your gifts and talents more fully but opportunities appear to be on hold, your time has not come yet to fully unveil what God has given you. Only God knows when the time is ripe to release what He has placed into your hands. His anointing is there, but it may not be the right time to move you forward yet. The way I see it is God gives us gifts and talents and when we give back to Him all that He has given to us, He develops and anoints our gifts and talents and then He gives them back to us to use for His glory.

God never slumbers nor sleeps and in His appointed time doors of opportunity open. His gifts and talents and anointing are given for a reason and scheduled for a definite season to reveal His glory. When it becomes hard to trust that God's plan will unfold during a season that seems endless, God is building in you all that you will need to sustain you once you arrive at your appointed destination. So at times when you don't understand a word or a promise He has spoken to your heart which appears in opposition to the life you are living now, seek God in prayer first and then join with a close friend or close family member if the need arises to pray through what you are walking through. I just so happened to read the other day words that pricked my heart that reveal the heart of God when it comes to those He loves—if God causes the grief you feel, surely He will have compassion according to His abundant lovingkindness.[6]

Humble ourselves under God's almighty hand and in due season we shall reap if we faint not the Word of God declares. Though not always easy, His word yields an abundance of ripe fruit. All the more reason to pray without ceasing and to make our requests known to God with thanksgiving. All the more reason to yield to the beat of God's heart. All the more reason to believe, apart from Him we can do nothing.[7] I've learned when it comes to changing things related to the way we live, some things don't need to be restored. They need to be transformed into something brand new.

The people God uses today are not unlike those He worked through during biblical times—people who had been broken and weary from experiencing one hardship after another. So don't lose hope. We don't have to look about in worrisome doubt when much needed connections are nowhere

6. Lamentations 3:32.
7. John 15:5.

in sight because God has a set time to set things in motion. Sometimes He saves the best for last. So don't lose your praise because praise is a weapon. And don't let anybody silence your song. Instead, call to mind that in due season we shall reap if we faint not. God always pulls His people out of a pit of despair to reach their appointed destiny. With the highs and lows of living life, sometimes our walk is interrupted though God continues to see and guide us through it all. Even in the hurtful places. In walking with God we find that He heals, He sets captives free, but He also allows suffering.

A good example of what I just wrote is to consider Moses who ran away from Egypt, and he spent 40 years in the wilderness before fulfilling his God-given assignment. And David, although anointed as king, did not ascend to the throne for roughly 20 years while he ran for his life from King Saul, suffering one distressing episode after another. And Joseph experienced his own time of solitude and heartache, while both men suffered betrayal. Betrayal is not new. Christ Himself suffered betrayal. This morning, God opened my eyes to arm us with this truth and to remind us of words written in Zechariah 13:6 when it declares, "And one will say to him, 'What are these wounds between your arms?' Then he will say, 'Those with which I was wounded in the house of my friends.'"

There is always a process and divine reason behind every season in life we go through. God intends for us to know that regardless of the season, we are whole and complete. He intends for us to take note of the uneasy sense we feel when something is off and to walk away from it. His desire is for us to learn from past mistakes and wrongful decisions so they are not repeated. He prepares us beforehand to walk successfully in places He has determined for our steps to venture into because we need to be equipped and ready once we arrive at the place where He is divinely guiding us to. So while we await God's timing to manifest His word, we may need to shift our mindset from despair to reassuring hope upon realizing that every thought doesn't need to occupy space in our minds. So go ahead and ask God to rekindle the small flicker of hope living inside your heart. Quoting C. S. Lewis when it comes to the hardships we encounter in life, "Hardships often prepare ordinary people for an extraordinary destiny."

> I Peter 5:10. After you have suffered for a little while, the God of all grace, who called you to His eternal glory in Christ, will Himself perfect, confirm, strengthen and establish you. (NASB95)

Added Note. Weeks after thinking I had completed this story, one morning my plan was to study something in the New Testament but the Holy Spirit directed me to the Book of Ezekiel, Chapter 12, Verse 28. Speaking about God's delay, this Scripture revealed to me an aspect about God's nature that I had not understood before. Here we read—"Therefore say to them, 'Thus says the Lord God, "None of My words will be delayed any longer. Whatever word I speak will be performed,"' declares the Lord God. (NASB95). Desiring to clearly understand Verse 28, I thought to myself, *I don't really think of God truly delaying* any *matter because the answer to our prayers will unfold in His perfect timing,* which is true. But here we find God acknowledging He *does* delay a matter when declaring that none of His words will be delayed any longer. How good it is for eyes to open to truths God reveals about His own character. I find these same words spoken by God in other places in the Bible which reminds me of the time I read in the Bible where God makes known He has a soul. Go ahead and search for it. Lastly, in Psalms 40 and 70, David cried out to God, "do not delay," and also Daniel voiced the same cry in Daniel 9:19, both men crying out for God's immediate delivering power. It is interesting to note when God speaks of a matter no longer being delayed, I discovered the intended meaning is things will happen quickly in the moment God moves on our behalf.

Growing Pains
Pulling My Little Red Wagon

Reflecting on another significant moment in my journey with God took place on the morning of May 15, 2011. Almost 14 years ago, in my spirit I heard God call me His daughter. Later this same morning while fellowshipping with a local church, to my surprise a woman was handed a microphone and she explained to the church what the term daughter means. She said using the word daughter is a term of endearment, and it is a big deal to be called daughter especially by the Savior. How timely is God in confirming His word to a listening heart. Every now and then, I go back to reread my handwritten note I wrote next to Verse 34 of Chapter Five in the Book of Mark because it was while reading this verse of Scripture, I heard God call me His daughter. When I look back from where I began to where I am today, I see God's hand of intervention, His timely revelation and protection when I didn't even know to invite Him in. I also recognize after reaching out to God and sometimes even faltering along the way, He continued being there for me by providing clear direction and most of all, His unfailing love.

The title *Pulling My Little Red Wagon* was birthed from an experience I had one Sunday morning during a worship service. While visiting a local church, I watched as the pastor strolled slowly towards the podium as he pulled a little red wagon behind him. The message he delivered stood out because it did not connect at all with the image of the little red wagon resting beside his feet while he stood at the podium. Nor could his message be found anywhere in the Bible. When I look across the memories of many unexpected places God took me to and through, and a few times unwillingly on my part, I see a plethora of struggles, some failures that served as teachers to guide me in learning lessons from life experiences not to be repeated. Some victories, many trials, places of brokenness, times of hanging by a thread, betrayal and loss. As I look back, I also see God's presence in every circumstance I encountered. The place in my heart that holds my life experiences call to mind God's delivering power and the change He has brought about in times of answered prayer, and in times of prayers in process. I reflect on God's delivering power in times of surrendering it all and in times of waiting when not surrendering enough. I see my personal relationship with the God who created the whole universe all wrapped up inside His perfect plan for my life that carries the fragrance of His presence, His grace, and His mercy and everything I know about Him all stretched across the fabric of my life story, which is symbolized by the title of this story, *Pulling My Little Red Wagon*. One thing I have learned about God is when He unfolds a promise, He does something tangible to let you know His timing is perfect. When He says a matter will no longer be delayed, it doesn't mean it will take place right at the moment. It means when the time is right, nothing can delay God's hand.

God doesn't leave us where we are and He doesn't waste any part of our journey either. Think of Peter's tarnished beginning as written in the New Testament. His stained beginning as he started out in life illustrates that we do have hope. Let me share a few encouraging stories packed inside my little red wagon.

For over 25 years now, I have written and published something about my journey with God which spans across 40 plus years which are filled with unexpected encounters and timely deliverances as I cried out to God in prayer. Recognizing that God takes us through something to bring us to something is worth writing it all down in some form so we remember our journey with Him, and share it with others. Like the time a few years ago when a young woman entered our job center. Although I wrote about her story in a previous book, it is worth mentioning again.

I saw her as she slowly ambled towards my office with her shoulders hunched over and her head bowed low and a look of defeat painted across her face. She strolled directly into my office and sat down in an empty seat and began to cry as she shared a story of betrayal at the hands of her supervisor who had gained her trust. As she spoke, her story revealed knowing God personally. It had to be God who gave me encouraging words to strengthen and uplift her heart when I told her that Satan desires to sift her like wheat, but she is a *mighty* woman of God. Upon hearing these words her eyes lit up as she thrusted her shoulders back while sitting quietly and attentively listening to liberating words God placed in my heart. A short time later, this young woman left from my office with a smile on her face and her head held high as she strutted in confidence through our lobby to exit the building. God sets the captives free and He uses you and me to do it.

On a different day, I noticed another young woman crying as she walked slowly towards an exit door at the unemployment center where I sometimes worked. Before reaching the door, I stopped her to ask what was wrong. She told me she was about to lose her apartment and she and her young son had no place to go. She shared her story of waiting on a call from the county, a call that would grant approval to sustain her housing. After listening to her story, immediately I prayed for God to intervene by allowing her to hear from the county on this same evening. I did not see this young woman for a few months, but when I saw her again she looked at me with a beaming smile as she reminded me of my prayer. She told me the very evening I prayed for her is the same evening she received the call from the county she had been waiting on to sustain housing for her and her young son. I believe anything can change when somebody prays because there is power in prayer. Be mindful of the words you speak because words give life.

Never will I forget the teenage boy I met while at work who I immediately perceived needed medical attention. This young lad I perceived was under such extreme pressure because each time we met, his face held an anguished look and he spoke through clenched teeth. As soon as I could on one of my lunch hours, I drove him to the local county building to register for medical care under his mother's name. We had to navigate the obstacles he faced to become registered, but sometime later when I saw him again, he no longer spoke through clenched teeth and the anguished look he had on his face was gone. Now there was a warm smile on his face as he shared with me he was considering enrolling in a training program. He also shared his life at home was better. There is something I remember about the time when I drove him to the county building to register for medical care. On the way out we happened to see one of his uncles who told me to leave this young boy in his care. Promising to keep him safe, although I really didn't like the look in this man's eyes because what I saw did not match his promise, but I left this young lad with him only to find out later his uncle didn't keep him safe at all.

Then there was the young man I saw leaning against the outside of a Dollar Tree store. Although I mentioned his story too in a previous book, thoughts of his thin frame and the frailness of his small dog still come to mind as I share meaningful life stories on my journey with God. Caught off guard when I saw his thin, frail body, and after buying him food, as I drove home, I couldn't stop the tears from flowing. I prayed for open doors to get him off the streets while pondering whether he had any close living relatives. How often we see this same situation though America is one of the richest countries in the world. I now understand why Christ said the poor will always be with us. I believe partly it was because He foresaw the heart of unyielding man who will not help those struggling to make it in life.

Something About Knowing God

God knows the place He is bringing us to from the places He has brought us from as we can see in Father Abraham's life story when God called him to leave his native land. As we travel to unfamiliar places, God sprinkles our lives with memorable moments and reserves a remnant of people who not only love Him, but will also walk alongside you. For the longest time in my own life story, God had me walking into unfamiliar territory as I reflect back to working inside an all-male prison. But I now realize that venture was meant for God to bring His light into a dark place where people need hope. Seasoned by trials and times when I questioned if I was going to make it, God came and brought me through each time as He continues to lead me to write His stories through this earthen vessel. Same as you, I am still reaching out to His outstretched hand.

This brings to mind a few more brief but meaningful encounters I had with God. One in particular took place on December 12, 1988. As already affirmed, I believe past histories and life experiences, especially those written on the pages of the Bible hold life lessons that can significantly impact life today because they lead us to understanding something more about knowing God and in recognizing that He knows best. This story took place while I was still young in the faith but determined to follow God through the darkest of times.

One day while feeling hopeless and helpless and talking to God, for the first time in my life, I heard God speak a Scripture to my heart for me to read. When I first heard it, I initially thought it was me talking to myself until I read the Scripture. The Scripture God spoke to my heart was Romans 8:28. The encouraging words spoken through Apostle Paul gave hope to my ailing heart during a very trying season of life. God knew exactly what I needed and He had come to provide for me. Though initially, I had written a note next to this Scripture in my Bible doubtfully claiming God had given it to me because I had never experienced anything like this, it was on the following day when it became clear to me it was God who had spoken to my heart. On the following day, I received a Christmas card from my old friend LaNetra and on the back of the envelope she had written the words "Romans 8:28" which was the very Scripture God had spoken to my heart the day before. Surely I had heard from God so I went back to my Bible to add another comment next to my doubtful handwritten note that states, "Everything would be all right, and everything was all right." God had felt my pain and He had come to encourage my heart. God's voice is not silent and He will use His inspired Word spoken through others in the Bible to speak to us today. This was my third epochal moment experienced with God. On another occasion God gave me a Scripture, but instead of speaking the Scripture to my heart He guided me to where it is found in the Bible. This time my situation had to do with a court case involving our family pet at a time when our neighbors did not speak the truth. God used the actions described in the ninth and tenth verses of this particular passage of Scripture[8] to speak to my heart exactly what I would later see unfolding right before my eyes the day I went to court. Although my knees trembled as I walked across the courthouse lawn, God still honored what He had spoken to my heart earlier despite me feeling fear. Looking back, I now understand something that takes place in the world today. We cross from grace to being judged for our personal choices as our decisions bring about consequences. The behaviors and the consequences I saw unfolding before my eyes that day in court were new to me but not new to God.

From other handwritten notes in my Bible, I saw where God brought me back to the same Scripture four different times. In March of 1987, because I kept going back to God about the same problem, He kept giving me the same answer. A few years later as turbulent trials continued to pummel my life, while sharing my plight with my old friend Carrie, she said to me, "Vera, you are chosen." And I told her I didn't want to be chosen because it was too hard. But after learning something more about knowing God, am I ever thankful to be one of His chosen vessels because God keeps us through every storm, every battle, and every setback. But He also uses setbacks to bring us through divinely appointed setups for our good. He opens our eyes to see what being chosen looks like as we experience His presence even in silent moments. Figuratively speaking, my little red wagon is packed full of life experiences that wrought wisdom, knowledge and understanding mostly from walking alone with God. Albeit brief, here are two more memorable real-life encounters.

Having prayed earnestly before accepting a new job, I did not understand why things quickly turned upside down from calming moments into a very disheartening and disturbing array of experiences. For the first time in my life, I questioned God's intent. Right after joining with this company, I was placed in a position I had never interviewed for nor was I told anything about it. Feeling trapped and deceived by God, I was so distraught I went to God in bewilderment and asked, "Do You know how I feel?!" And He led me straight to Jeremiah Chapter 20, Verse 7 where Jeremiah cried

---

8. Psalm 5:8–12. (NASB95).

out the very same concern when he lamented, "O Lord, Thou hast deceived me, and I was deceived. Thou has overcome me and prevailed. I have become a laughingstock all day long; everyone mocks me." Yes, God knew exactly how I felt, and I had to learn as Jeremiah did, God doesn't deceive. His purpose for me accepting this new position was to provide finances to cover a small window of time for my young family. Two weeks later on the heels of this trying experience, God opened the door to a secure position that lasted 14 years and one with better pay and benefits. I had not learned yet that God works out everything for our good no matter how bad it looks in the beginning. Everything we go through is to build our trust in God and to lay a foundation that is not easily shaken. From more handwritten notes in my Bible, what I wrote on July 23, 1992, serves as a constant reminder—God always has the best in mind for those who follow closely after Him.

There were many times back in the 90's and one in particular when the enemy used a co-worker sitting in a cubicle directly behind me to report to HR simple things I would do that were weaponized against me. Barely above a whisper, I would sing praise songs to God while working at my desk. Pretending to need something, this co-worker would enter my cubical and stand right next to my desk catching me off guard while she listened to my whispered songs of praise. She joined hands with our department manager and together they both worked against me to the point my former Pastor Gainey described what I was going through as real persecution. But God won for me in the end reigning in power which I disclose in my book *When God Spoke To Me, He Said* . . . You will be surprised to learn what happened later on to the leadership team at this company. God knows just how to humble a proud heart.

God moves the immovable. Although the trials that impacted my life have been more than enough for me and a number of them I certainly did not want to experience, everything we go through resounds with this guiding truth I believe we all need to remember—"Beloved, do not think it strange concerning the fiery trial which is to try you, as though some strange thing happened to you."[9] Sometimes when we feel what lies ahead is more than we can bear and we cry out to God it is enough now Lord, we've done all we can do to stand faithfully, be encouraged by a few insightful words spoken by the late Doctor Charles Stanley when he asserted—"Whether you're taking a stand for righteousness or navigating difficult times with godly patience, be mindful of His wisdom. Because God knows the future

---

9. I Peter 4:12 (NJKV).

and allows our hardships, you can trust Him to handle the consequences of your faithfulness."[10]

Starting out as a very timid and shy little girl who loved writing, never did I perceive God would use my love for writing as a major part of my life journey, my purpose. The struggles I share in my opening poem were real starting with the tragic death of my young and beautiful pregnant mother and then going on to raise a family on my own. And in the midst of it all, I was answering the call of God placed upon my life which was unknown to me at this time and would later lead to a cross-country journey with a younger brother of mine. Young kids with younger kids traveling alone with God overseeing it all is what I see now.

Had God not taken me through such trying seasons in life and brought me safely out on the other side, had He not often led me to Scriptures that spoke to my heart as I grew in my faith, I would not know His name as I know it now. And I would not understand up close and personal attributes about His presence, His undying love, His voice, His silence, and the God who fights for me. I would not know the God who brings blessings out of tragedy, treasures out of ashes from things discarded and thrown away. No matter what you may be facing or have gone through in the past; no matter if you are still waiting for the dust to settle from regretful moments experienced not so long ago, as Jesus spoke to the synagogue official, I repeat His words back to you—"Do not be afraid any longer, only believe."[11]

> Hosea 6:1. Come, let us return to the Lord, for He has torn us, but He will heal us; He has wounded us, but He will bandage us.
>
> I Corinthians 2:16. For who has known the mind of the Lord that he should instruct Him? But we have the mind of Christ. (NASB95)

---

10. In Touch Ministries. Your daily devotion for 08/07/2024. Inspired by The Teachings of Charles F. Stanley. "Embracing Your Fiery Trials."

11. Mark 5:36 (NASB95).

Something About Knowing God

Seeing Through His Eyes

Only God can open the eyes of spiritual blindness. Only God can restore health to the body, and only God can manifest something that wasn't there before. Only God can set the captives free and He often uses you and me. Only God can breathe life into words written over two thousand years ago that continue to penetrate listening hearts today.

For the third time in a ten-year period, God led me again to the same verse of Scripture that pierced my heart just as it did on two earlier occasions. You would think I should have understood by now what God was communicating to me the first time He led me here on March 22, 1989, but I didn't. Because of the intensity of the storms I was facing, the only thing I could see was misery. If God's intent was to remove things I no longer needed, I couldn't see it because the trials hammering my life were just too fierce. So about ten years later on April 26, 2000, God brought me back to this same Scripture. Still I didn't get it. But when I look back some 35 years later, I think it may have been somewhere around the third time when I began to see a bit more about what God intended for me to understand over the passing years. The third time happened on Mother's Day, May 14, 2000. This time when God led me to this Scripture, I finally saw it. It was as though the words called out to me personally when I read—"Then Eliphaz the Temanite answered, 'Behold you have admonished many, and you have strengthened weak hands. Your words have helped the tottering to stand, and you have strengthened feeble knees. But now it has come to you, and you are impatient; it touches you and you are dismayed.' "[12] God had been talking to me all along about my own life story.

Who can declare without error God will not speak a message today from words specifically directed to someone in the Bible written thousands of years ago? When God determines to open the eyes of one of His servants, He alone chooses the means to communicate His spiritual truths. From experiencing other similar situations, I understand God will give words of clear direction, correction, and encouragement through someone else's life story printed out on the pages of the Bible as His word is alive and sharper than any two-edged sword. Whether God leads one of His chosen servants to a Scripture to bring awareness to unlearned or unchecked behaviors or in times of experiencing distressing moments where hope is needed, God continues to extend His arm of care through biblical passages

---

12. Job 4:3–5. (NASB95).

and specific Scriptures, or through whatever mode of communication He chooses which can involve His creation in many insightful ways as Jesus did in His parables or He uses someone or something familiar, and at times something totally unexpected and totally unfamiliar.

Written thousands of years ago, prayers of guidance and prayers of thanksgiving and reminders of God's power to redeem us in trying moments are recorded throughout the pages of the Bible that we continue to learn from today. Because God can speak through a donkey and because He can make the rocks cry out, who can put God in a box and determine all His ways? Whatever means of communication God chooses to use to speak through, I try my best to listen. Consider that God spoke to the heart of kings in the Bible who did not even know His name. So who of us can say with certainly how God will and won't speak? I think we sometimes minimize God's voice though always we should exercise discernment which is vital.

Now back to the times God led me to read Eliphaz the Temanite's outspoken statement. The first time, He led me here came about as a result of turbulent twists and turns taking place while I was still employed in the corporate world. The second time God pierced my heart when He led me back to this same Scripture was because I wanted to know how He felt about me sharing with Him my heartfelt feelings concerning a person who had betrayed my trust. The third time God led me to this Scripture, the scribbly handwritten notes in my Bible read, "I just got done reflecting on my horror of attaching myself to . . ." (name withheld). Although my purpose in seeking God these three times concerned different reasons, they all brought about the same measure of suffering. God not only desired for me to understand He was aware of the difficult times I was facing, but He also wanted me to see He was still using me to help others with their own life struggles. This reveals something about God's heart. Our own troubles should not stop us from showing compassionate care for others. I believe it was Chuck Swindoll who said, "In the hardest of times, you can produce some of your best works." And thankfully we can realize as recently shared by Pastor Steven Furtick, "Every season of suffering has an expiration date."[13]

I am thankful for the many opportunities God brings my way to encourage and lift up in prayer the needs and concerns of others and for the opportunities to do something tangible when I can. Occasionally, God would open a door only for me to pray for someone and I would

---

13. Online sermon. *Overwhelmed by Life's Demands*. 10/15/2024.

immediately see a change in their countenance, and later on become aware of a change in their condition. Helping others is the reason I believe we are here. To encourage and to help strengthen others as they walk this journey. To help set people free from yokes and chains binding them and not merely looking out for our own personal interests, but for the interests of others[14] which brings to mind a host of relatable real-life stories included in my book *From His Heart To My Heart, A Wilderness Journey*.

Hard times make us cry out while sometimes it seems we go through situations that do not appear to touch the lives of those around us. This reminds me of something I shared with my youngest son when he about twelve years old. One day, I told him how badly I was feeling, and I said I wasn't going to tell God. He looked at me and said, "Mom, God heard what you said so He knows how you feel." Yep, that was me being a bit naive to say such a thing, but sometimes you've cried out for so long over the same issue and nothing seems to have changed so you are forced let go and let God have His way. This reminds me of the story of Hannah in the Old Testament.

Hannah cried out year after year because of her desire to give birth to a child. In Hannah's day, it was a shameful thing not to be able to give birth so Hannah cried out until God answered her prayer. God's answer came through the high priest named Eli, but God doesn't always use someone else to bring His answer to you. He speaks to our own heart and spirit too.

Maturity has brought about trusting God when I am tired, and when I can't see what lies ahead, and while waiting on God to turn my circumstances around. We come to a place of recognizing God's presence and walking in His peace when His timing takes longer than we think. We come to the place of rejoicing in His presence praising His great name when we believe He has a divine purpose for the battles taking place around us which I believe is key to standing while awaiting His time of deliverance. Think of closed doors as God's divine intervention to protect and take to heart these encouraging words, "The Lord is good to those who wait for Him, to the person who seeks Him."[15]

Change is coming though we don't see it yet is what I say. God has taught me that I can trust in His promises and also to appreciate when He arrives. No matter how it looks today, His arrival is always the best time to come through even when He delays a matter.

14. Philippians 2:3–4. (NASB95).
15. Lamentations 3:25 (NASB95).

Growing Pains

Psalm 71:16. I will come and proclaim your mighty acts, Sovereign Lord; I will proclaim your righteous deeds, Yours alone. (NIV)

Jeremiah 32:27. Behold, I am the Lord, the God of all flesh; is anything too difficult for Me? (NASB95)

Something About Knowing God

Yet Will I Hope in Him

In the previous story you just read, I mentioned trusting God, and I do, but before I got here, there is a story worth telling. The other day, I just so happened to run across more handwritten notes in my Bible dated June 28th, 1992, some 30 years ago. This is my story:

Boy, did I ever regret saying those words! While talking on the phone with an old friend, I said them. And immediately she blurted out, "Don't say that because Betty did and look what's happening to her!" Her sister Betty was getting tore up from the floor up as we used to say, and it all seemed to have started right after she boldly proclaimed the same words of Job that I had just boisterously asserted —"Though He slay me, yet will I trust in Him."[16] All three of us were going through some really tough times and if I thought my life was unraveling before I spoke Job's words, things really went downhill afterwards. Things went south so quickly, I could barely stand.

About a month later on July 24th, because my suffering was so intense, I kept asking God why was all this happening to me, and He led me straight to the very words of Job I had boldly declared over the phone to my friend. Two days after proclaiming Job's words my friend said she thought all the many things happening in my life was because I had spoken of trusting God no matter what.

Well, I have since learned that God not only hears the words we speak, but He takes them to heart. As I look back many years later, I believe God was testing my faith when I confessed Job's words. I had boldly proclaimed that I trust Him and He was testing the very words I declared. I now recognize when I spoke those words, I did not understand the depth of their meaning as I understand them today. I had spoken words without forethought, and it didn't take long for God to remind me He heard what I said. As a result of the overwhelming events that unfolded right after repeating Job's words, it would be years before I would repeat these same words again let alone voice them quietly to myself. Whenever I would read the Book of Job, I would skip right over them. Needless to say, I have learned the importance of staying mindful of the words we allow to come out of our mouths because words have power. God hears, and He tests the heart. Before publishing this book, my heart was so pricked with concern that for the first time some 30 years later, I happened to hear a well-known pastor

---

16. Job Chapter 13, Verse 15. (NIV).

boastfully proclaim these same words of Job. I must admit my heart sank a bit as my mind raced back to the time when I spoke these very same words. I can only hope and pray this well-known pastor knew exactly what he was saying to God. Lord, help us not to speak words without knowledge.

It is amazing to me some 30 years after having understood that trials will always be a part of life which is clearly pointed out in John, Chapter 16, Verse 33, to now knowingly confess to God concerning the most precious desires of my heart, "Lord, Your will be done" is growth. I lay it all down. Though the Bible tells us to make our requests known to God, releasing the outcome to God speaks volumes about our maturity and trust if we truly believe the words we speak. It follows the example of Christ when He was nailed to the cross and He asked for His Father's will to be done over His own heartfelt request. What I see as I write this book is by Jesus laying down His own desire to accept the will of the Father resulted in the greatest gift for all mankind—our salvation. I made the comment about Jesus laying down His own desire for God's will during a recent prayer team call and it stirred the heart of the sister leading the prayer call to share an edifying thought about a seed falling to the ground must die before it bears fruit.[17] I believe this happens in your life and in my life. We must die to self-will in order to fulfill God's sovereign will.

I strive to keep a watchful eye on allowing my own expectations to get ahead of me as I wait upon the Lord. I have learned the wisdom in confessing, "Lord, help me to accept what I cannot change." While understanding that God can be trusted with everything that concerns you and me, I also know if we find ourselves slipping in trusting God fully, recalling His past deliverances keeps us focused and firmly rooted in trusting Him again and again.

Before concluding this story, a thought arose about a man who long ago expressed his own heartfelt sentiments to God just as I had done when I repeated Job's words. This man's words appear to me to have been spoken without much forethought just as I had done. The man I am referring to is Jephthan and his story is written in the Book of Judges. Here we find Jephthan proclaiming to the Lord, "If Thou wilt indeed give the sons of Ammon into my hand, then it shall be that whatever comes out of the doors of my house to meet me when I return in peace from the sons of Ammon, it shall be the Lord's, and I will offer it up as a burnt offering."[18] Thankfully

---

17. John 12:24 (NASB95).
18. Judges Chapter 11, Verses 30–31. (NASB95).

the intent of Jephthah's words according to my Bible's footnotes can be translated "shall surely be the Lord's (if a human being comes first), or I will offer it up for a burnt offering (if an animal appears first)."[19] Read Jephthah's story to find out just how deeply he felt when he saw his daughter was first to come out from the door of his house to meet him.

Every word we speak whether to God or to man ought to be carefully weighed. As God heard the words of Jephthan over two thousand years ago, He hears the words we speak to Him today. He hears the words we voice to others which cannot be separated from reflecting on our personal relationship with Him. Our words should be filtered through His Holy Spirit.

> Psalm 141:3. Set a guard, O Lord, over my mouth; keep watch over the door of my lips. (NKJV)
>
> Proverbs 17:3. The refining pot is for silver and the furnace for gold, but the Lord tests the hearts. (NKJV)
>
> Zechariah 13:9. Refine them as silver is refined, and test them as gold is tested. They will call on My name, and I will answer them; I will say, 'They are My people,' and they will say, 'The Lord is my God.' (NASB95)

---

19. Judges Chapter 11:31 (NASB95).

My God, My Healer

I revisit the memory of my mother's untimely death because God has shown me He is my Healer. My mother's gentle and caring nature was clearly evident in the eyes of her earthy father because he called her his lamb. I remember being told when he learned about her death he kept repeating, "Not my lamb, not my lamb." So hard on him was her unimaginable death, he didn't attend her funeral. I don't think he could bear to face seeing the man who took his precious daughter's life. It was probably best for my grandpa not to witness the frightened look on my mother's face that could not be erased by the funeral home workers. Though too young to understand it all, in spite of everything, I grew up loving the only earthly father I ever had. I believe we all did. So although he took our mother's life, I wanted him to live.

While writing this book, I just so happened to run across more handwritten notes in my Bible from 1985. This was a time when I questioned God concerning my dad's health. The day I questioned God about his health, I was led by the Holy Spirit to a specific word in the Bible which spoke directly to my heart that addressed the issue I was facing. The Scripture I was led to read was Romans 13: 11.[20] Directly above this Scripture, I had written: "April 1985—my dad was sick and doctors didn't know if he was going to come out of his coma. I asked God was He going to let my daddy die. Answer, 'No,' He'd awaken him from his coma! This very hour, my dad came to." God had answered my prayer ahead of hearing from the doctors. I loved the only dad I ever knew.

During most of my growing up years, the memory of seeing my mother as I last saw her, I grew afraid to sleep in a darkened room. For many years, I had to keep a light on because the thought of seeing my mother propped up against the end of my parents bed persisted in my thoughts. This is where my dad left her and this is where she and the baby growing inside her died. So two people died before my eyes on this tragic day, but only one of them did I ever come to know in the first seven years of my life. How good it is to learn God's truth—to be absent from the body is to be present with the Lord.[21]

---

20. Romans 13:11. "And this do, knowing the time, that it is already the hour for you to awaken from sleep; for now salvation is nearer to us than when we believed."

21. Second Corinthians 5:8.

Something About Knowing God

As a youngster, people used to stop and stare as I passed by them on a sidewalk. I would stop to glance behind me because I could sense their gaze and then I would see them whispering. I would catch them standing still, pointing a finger as they stared at me. As mentioned earlier, what happened to my mother over 60 years ago was an uncommon occurrence so it shocked our small community. While attending school, my heart was always pained when Mother's Day came around. And for a long time during my growing up years, I would cry out for her, telling her how much I missed her and needed her here. And every year on her birthday anniversary, I remember to tell her happy birthday. I told myself when I reach the age of 42, I would look at myself in the mirror to see just how young my mother really was when she departed this earth. On my 42nd birthday, I looked in the mirror and was alarmed to realize just how young my mother really was when she died. My mother was stopped short of living the years of a fruitful life. Stopped short of seeing her children and her grandchildren grow up. It took years, but one day I told myself because of the way she suffered in an unhealthy marriage, she was better off being with the Lord, but not the way she died.

My dad lived on for many years after the death of my mother. His family hired the best attorney to fight for his freedom whose name I still remember. There were those back then who recognized the sting left behind the tragedy my dad caused. For one, the steel foundry where he worked did not want to take him back after he returned home from jail. But through the help of his well-known attorney, the foundry was forced to give him back his job.

About 20 years ago, I called one of my sisters and shared with her I had suddenly remembered the pain I carried with me all those years behind our mother's death. And I told her I was looking all over my body as if searching for an open sore, but I couldn't find it anymore. Immediately, she responded, "Why are you looking for it?" As if to say what I was doing makes no sense at all. I think she spoke without knowledge because in my eyes, I saw clearly that day that God was showing me I was healed. The scar was no longer there. The pain was no longer a lingering part of my life. Without knowing to ask God to heal me, He graciously healed me anyway. He knew what I needed in order to move me forward on my life's journey.

Although the memory of my mother will always remain with me, no longer will be the invisible wound so often a constant companion in the lives of many hurting and traumatized people. Over the years I have learned sometimes the one who is supposed to love you is the one responsible for your greatest pain. God brings healing, but at times He allows suffering and even death. He is able to bring us through it all as we place our trust in Him. He saw it all before we got to where we are today.

If you've been abused, mis-used, traumatized as a child or as a young person saturate your heart with this truth—whatever happened to you was not your fault. It was the other person's choice to behave the way they did so don't immerse yourself in counter-productive thoughts that will only hold you captive. God sees all and we never get away. Sometimes we just get by for a season, but we never get away. There are consequences we face as a result of our behaviors.

If you brought harm to someone's life because of your own unabated life choices, confess the wrong done to that person, and repent. Don't expect them to go on as if nothing happened because something did happen, and some things we go through are life changing. As the Word of God declares, what we've done to the least of them we've done those things unto Him. We cannot separate our relationship with God from how we treat others. We have free will, but God provides His wisdom to make the decision to turn away from anything that does not benefit life. We can resist the enemy when we submit ourselves first unto God. If what we are doing does not reflect God's heart, we bind it in the name of Christ Jesus and we apologize because confession heals. We repent and strive to serve others in a spirit of love. Today, make the choice to choose God and to choose nurturing relationships that recognize your value. Don't break yourself trying to get others to change. Understand that when it comes to genuine love, you should not only be found useful, but valuable too.

If you happen to be someone living with regret or shame because of poor life choices, or you remind yourself of things you should have done better after coming to know God personally, God is your Healer. He knows where you are and His grace pardons. Pray to Him while understanding some things only come about by way of prayer *and* fasting. Strive to surrender your heart completely to His will. Be careful not to rely on your own strength alone because the very nature of flesh is flesh, and flesh will only take you so far. Remember as Christ declared in the Bible, "Apart from Me, you can do nothing."[22]

There are certain memories that remain vivid in my mind when my mother died. Seeing the tears and the pain etched across the face of two of

---

22. John 15:5.

my older sisters when they came home after being told mama was dead. The ambulance that came and took our mother away for the last time, I remember. Having been told it took at least two times for the highway patrolmen to believe my dad's story when he stopped them on the freeway to tell them that he killed his wife. Being asked to take the witness stand and hearing the judge say to take me down from the witness stand because he said I was too nervous. There are other details tucked away in my memory, but one thing I often wished is that she had not told our dad of her plan to leave. Just because someone is your spouse, it doesn't make them mature enough to handle what you know.

Healing is a process. Sometimes the process of healing is long. Sometimes, shorter. Healing is personal too so no one can tell you not to hurt behind something that shattered your life or was life changing for you. What you went through is something *you* walked through, not them. Whatever scarred you as a child, as a young adult or even now, God is your Healer. If you are struggling with relational or health issues or an addiction or rejection, abandonment issues or not seeing yourself the way God sees you as whole and complete while you weigh the opinions of others, or if you are struggling with undeserved pain or something entirely different, cling to God above all else because He's got you. He knows where He is taking you in your spiritual development in order for you to leave behind what needs to be left behind. Choose to be around those with a heart after God. Choose people who are striving to live for God and to honor God in the friendship where both people will hold fast to biblical principles. Realize that every opportunity for friendship is not always from the hand of God. The enemy has a hand too so don't go where you know you will be tempted to relive something or to be with someone who hurts your life. Don't just choose what looks good, what feels good. Instead choose what is God. If His presence is not there, you shouldn't be there either. Learning from watching a close friend struggle, certain relationships can set up anxiety and restlessness if we don't choose relationships that reflect God's presence in the close connections we establish. Placing God first in heart and mind is the foundational part of our journey.

Something else important to do is to carve out time to study the Bible. When we have the Word of God living inside us, meditating on Scripture hides His Word in our heart so it will there when we need it. Get involved in discipleship training if needed, and make the decision to set your heart on truly believing. Strive to apply God's word in every situation, small or great, that arises in life. Make up your mind to seek after God instead of indulging in things of the flesh that can only bring temporary pleasure. Something I read in my Bible footnotes[23] which should be applied in moments of temptation is contained in the meaning behind James 4:7–10 when my footnotes state, "There are 10 verbs, all commands, in these verses, in a tense which indicates the need for a decisive and urgent break with the old life."

Trust that God knows what to do with hurting experiences. Understand that sometimes you can hurt and don't even know to ask God to heal you just as it happened with me, and He heals you anyway. From spending time alone in God's presence and submissively listening to His voice, I have learned something about the author and finisher of my faith. His ears, His heart, and His eyes are inclined towards those who suffer. Father God, I thank You for continuing to speak to me about things I did not know and things I had forgotten until now. Thank you for others' life stories being a part of my journey to help shape what we all have in common. I thank you for moving me forward in my faith to believe. And I thank You, God, for Your power to heal and Your heart's intent to increase our faith to believe. Your daughter, Vera.

> Psalm 3:3. But You, O Lord, are a shield about me, my glory and the One who lifts my head. (NASB95)
>
> Isaiah 65:24. It will also come to pass that before they call, I will answer; and while they are still speaking, I will hear. (NASB95)

---

23. New American Standard Bible.

Something About Knowing God

In The Midst of it All

It is a good thing when experiencing the ups and downs of life to find joy where it can be found not only for our emotional and spiritual well-being but to tie families and other loved ones together. In the midst of dealing with life's challenges we can become so bogged down, so consumed with the seriousness of daily life we can forget how important it is to stop and smell the roses. While managing the pressures of life, sometimes we lose our focus in remembering God holds the details of our life in His hand. We sometimes forget to pause to breathe in refreshing and memorable past and present moments we've shared with close family, old friends, and neighbors, and the valued interactions we share with strangers we meet along the way. These precious moments paint a smile across our face as we reflect on joyous occasions in the midst of it all. Remembering old road trips is a good one that can bring heartfelt memories to life. Here's one of mine.

When my brother and I drove to California over 40 years ago, in the wee hours of the morning, both of us were wide awake because of our dread in facing the tallest mountain we'd ever faced—Mount Raton! That night we couldn't sleep a wink because all we ever knew about driving was driving on flat level ground. So it only took my brother Buddy one time to barely whisper in the wee hours of the morning, "Vera, are you awake?" "Yeah," I quickly but quietly whispered back so as not to awake my sleeping children. Both my brother and I were caught up in the moment of envisioning Mount Raton which in our minds eye looked as if it almost touched the sky! So in the wee hours of the morning neither one of us could sleep a wink because of the battle raging in our minds as we envisioned ourselves driving up and up the steep side of Mount Raton! But something else happened to squeeze every ounce of nerve we were holding onto. The next morning, would you believe while driving up this monstrous mountain all traffic was brought to a screeching halt! And there we sat carting such a heavy load, the body of my car almost touched the ground. Too young to realize the importance of not driving with such a heavy load, the shocks wore out in a matter of a few days of driving. When given the okay that morning, we kept driving up and up and up and now here we sat on the uphill side of a mountain that seemed to lean us backwards. But my old Chrysler did its thing without fail! Holding in place its brakes and all while humming a serious tune as it worked to climb this massive mountain with everything in tow! We couldn't wait to start driving again from the place of being stopped

Growing Pains

on such a massive incline though we drove in complete silence trying not to focus on the high slopes with very low or no guard rails at all. I watched my young brother nervously take a single puff on a new lite cigarette and then immediately crush it in the ash tray only to quickly and nervously murmur, "Vera, light me another one!" All I could do was to do as he mumbled as I lit one cigarette after another while I watched him handle Mount Raton all by himself. Couldn't help him at all because heights is not my thing. *But only if I have to*, I told myself. Once the wheels of that old Chrysler with the landau top touched flat ground, our eyes instantly locked onto each other while we let out an exhausting sigh of relief! We could hardly belief we made it across another mountain coming from the flat lands we were used to! Sometimes we still look back and laugh at the memory of him bravely driving up and over high Mount Raton! And by the way, we had stopped along the way because of fretting to drive cross any mountains and was told if we drove the route pointed out to us, we wouldn't have to drive over *any* mountains at all. We believed it, but it's not possible when driving to the West Coast from the Midwest or driving from the East Coast! And just so you know, my brother long ago relinquished his nicotine habit!

As the Bible declares, laughter is good for the soul so it is good to set in motion what is made known to us in the Bible to do. Even in spontaneous moments, we can find joy worth keeping. Here is another moment to enjoy from an incident that took place recently.

The other day, my oldest grandson and I were out walking and just like that I tumbled forward from a crack in the sidewalk. To keep myself from completely falling forward, what did I do but instantly reach out to grab hold to the back of my grandson's pants. Startled and in a quick flash he turned around and looked at me and said, "Grandma! What happened?! You could have pulled my pants down and everybody would have seen my boxers! It's a good think I had my pants tied tight around my waist!" (chuckle, chuckle!) Yes, it's a good thing he didn't leave the tie to his pants loosely tied or even left undone. Needless to say, after sharing with him the tip of my shoe met the uneven crack in the sidewalk and after letting out a sigh of relief, we laughed after thinking of all the people around us who would have seen his colorful boxers! And now that I think about it, God prepared us for this moment because my hard yank on the back of my grandson's pants kept me from falling, and because my grandson had tied the string on his pants tightly around his waist, his pants didn't budge a wink! God truly has a sense of humor!

Something About Knowing God

This next story is for sure what I describe as a "God moment." Before driving from up north to where home is now, of all things, my car broke down directly in front of my house. Having prepared my house to sell, I shared with the buyer's realtor about my car breaking down and she replied, "God had your car break down in front of your house and not on the highway. What a blessing!" Now comes the part of my story that brings an enjoyable and laughing "God moment." After having my car towed to the dealership, I heard God speak to my spirit, "Your car will be ready to roll." *Ready to Roll? God doesn't talk like that,"* I told myself. *"This must be me talking to myself."* But after my car was repaired, while waiting in the dealership lobby for the service manager to come speak to me about my car repairs, do you know what were the first words that came out of his mouth? "Your car is ready to roll!" In this incredibly moment, all I could think about were the words I heard spoken to my spirit earlier in the morning, and I knew beyond a shadow of doubt it was God who spoke those words to me. My car was indeed ready to roll! Like I said, God truly has a sense of humor! And sometimes He will use the very words that are most familiar to us to speak to us!

Years ago—can't do it now, but I jumped over a three foot tall retainer wall surrounding my front yard. As I knelt down gardening, I just so happened to hear the paws of a dog hitting the pavement, and looking up, I saw this huge mountain of a dog running straight towards me while its owner jogged energetically by its side. Seeing the dog's leash held limply in my neighbor's hand, without thinking, I quickly stood up and leaped right over that retainer wall! I didn't wait to hear what most people say about their dog, "Oh, he won't bite." My first thought was to aim for my unlocked screened front door. Though I stumbled across my front lawn, I latched onto my doorknob with a quickness and stood safely behind my front door screen. "Oh, he won't bite," my neighbor casually sang out as she jogged gingerly down the street. All I could see was this dog's monstrous size with his mouth hanging open as he galloped his long legs headed straight towards me! I can laugh now, but not back then!

Same thing happened to my neighbor down the street when he was outside gardening too. Lost in the sweet art of gardening, he did not hear this dog galloping across his front lawn straight towards him. In a heightened tone, my neighbor shared with me that his adrenaline hit the roof when he turned his head around only to look straight inside the mouth of a Great Dane! Downright scary but no harm done other than to scare the bejabbers out of us both! After sharing his story, I thought to myself, *My next door neighbor's dog would probably have only done to me the same thing it did to my neighbor which was to breathe his hot breath on the back of my unsuspecting neighbor's neck!*

What memories, what kodak moments do you have to refresh and warm your heart? God always brings opportunities for laughter to interrupt an otherwise busy day. It's like another time many years ago, I remember our Chaplain's Roast which was held on a nearby air force base. Chaplain Ewing confidently placed me in charge of the kids performing the Roast. Everything the youth shared led to ripples of laughter. But something they shared did not go over well with Chaplain Ewing! Though I no longer remember the roasting remark, I do remember the alarmed look on Chaplain Ewing's face when he glanced my way which seemed to say, "Oh, no, you didn't allow those kids to say what I just heard!" But I did, and they did! Everybody roared with laughter except for Chaplain Ewing! Must have been quite a loaded roasting remark because the look on his face told it all! I hope one day you read this book, Chaplain Ewing because no harm intended. Only moments to tickle the heart with joyous laughter! I wonder if Chaplain Roasts are now a thing of the past. A couple more delightful moments to share and I will end this humorous story.

I guess you know by now high places are definitely not for me, but only if I have to. After Mount Raton, would you believe I experienced two other incidents that jarred my senses to reaffirm what I just said! One time, my friend asked me to go camping with her and her family. Now I did ask her beforehand about the drive to where we were going and no problem at all she assured me. Looking back, I know she thought she understood what driving across high roads looked like to me, but sometimes we can see the same thing yet have an entirely different outlook, and this is just what happened. As we inched closer to our destination, the road suddenly changed. Glancing out the window to my right, I noticed a steep incline without any guard rails. It looked to me like a small mountain. After pointing towards it, I asked if we had to drive up that part of the road and she replied, "Mm-hmm," and with that said, my mouth instantly dropped open but not a single word came out. Only a bellowing "Ahhhh!" which I yelled at the top of my lungs that instantly stopped all conversations in the car. My friend's brother-in-law sitting in the back seat was already nervous because of the ascent we had previously mastered so I thought he would be the one screaming because of the jittery look in his eyes and the nervous smile plastered across his face and the visible beads of sweat forming on his forehead. But my roaring yell silenced his scream. The thought invading my mind was how on earth would the car we were riding in fit on the narrow and steep ledge to our right *and* while driving without any guard rails! But Satan IS a liar because we made it up the steep incline with no guard rails and all. Acknowledging healthy fear is one thing, but letting our mind drift away, I know, is another! Don't mind flying in an airplane though, but not my thing on the ground. *Only if I have to*, I always tell myself.

In frightful encounters, God continues to let me know, "I got you!" Even while working on completing this book, what did I need to do but take an elevator ride up to the 15th floor to meet with my new dentist. The first time inside the elevator I felt a bit unnerved but I wasn't going to allow this to stop me from reaching my destination. Two weeks later, I had to return to the same office and this time, I didn't feel much of anything at all. On this second trip, I spoke out loud to a perfect stranger as I told him my inner thoughts as I confessed I didn't like heights, and surprisingly he replied, "I don't either!" Told him I could fly though. "How 'bout you?" I asked. The intense shaking of his head and the tight smirk beaming across his lips clearly spoke the words, "Definitely NO!" I had to smile as I thought to myself, *I am not alone!* Although not caring much for heights, this stranger courageously rode to the 16th floor! We do it on shaky knees if we have to! That's what courage is. Doing it afraid if we have to!

One last climbing the high roads' experience I think we can all smile about. When my oldest grandson was about five years old, the church family I was a part of planned a camping trip, and because I love camping, I wanted my grandson to enjoy his first camping trip. Before signing up for the trip, I made sure to ask the pastor about the drive to the camping site. "Any high places to cross?" "Nope, none at all!" Relieved, I signed up for the camping trip. Driving alone with my grandson, no problem. But then came the mountain the pastor said would not be there! With no place to turn around, I drove up and up and up, and all but scrapped the paint off the side of my car as I hugged the mountainside while glancing out at trees that appeared the size of toothpicks. In this terrifying moment, I held it together because of the love and the safety I felt for my grandson. Boy was I relieved when the wheels of my car finally touched flat ground! While driving up the mountain, I would glance in the rearview mirror to see my grandson's smiling face, and God used his little smiling face to anchor my faith to keep me moving forward. You may as well know, somebody else had to drive my car back down the mountainside. Now that my grandson is older, he knows driving to high places is not my cup of tea! Only if I have to. In realizing the kind of fear that shifts our focus onto the circumstances we face instead of keeping our faith focused on God, I thank God for mustard seed size faith to move us forward in uncharted territory.

When it comes to challenging moments, some I have mastered and for others I am still growing, same as for you. I don't believe we ever stop growing and if we do, look out! Amid everything we face in life, God delights us with warm memories and many unexpected and joyful moments during our most challenging times. He doesn't omit times to pause to reflect on fond memories filled with irreplaceable moments to suddenly realize His protection is always there during unexpected moments when we're not sure where we're headed. God is letting us know that enjoying moments of laughter is just that important to our well-being!

> Proverbs 17:22. A cheerful heart is good medicine, but a crushed spirit dries up the bones. (NIV)

Added Note: I think it rather peculiar in the midst of writing spiritually grounded books, God shifted my writing projects momentarily from a spiritual path to write about laughter that warms the heart in my book *A Hilarious Moment!* which is a book filled with whimsical real-life stories of old school ways that worked. Truly it is good for the heart to find and reserve moments to enjoy joyous laughter with family and friends and others we meet along the way!

No Fear?

Nehemiah spoke of fear in the Fifth Chapter in the Book of Nehemiah, but the fear he spoke about had do with reverence for God. But then in Chapter Six, Nehemiah spoke several times of his own natural fear which came about soon after he spoke encouraging words to others not to be afraid as we read about in Chapter Four. But if we go back to an even earlier chapter, in Chapter Two, Verse Two, it is recorded here that Nehemiah confessed, "Then I was very much afraid." Sometimes what we sense is a valid reason to fear an impending situation, so natural fear is real and necessary. It can give us the focus we need to avoid harm. A fight or flight response is the body's automatic reaction to a threatening situation. So natural fear in some form or another touches all life if we will admit it. But as we would probably also agree, disabling fear can stop you in your tracks. Yet God says to fear not. But still we do fear. So fear must have a deeper meaning than we once thought, especially when it comes to people who God leads into new and unchartered territories. Not only are we to recognize gripping fear which comes to invade our inner peace, but perhaps we are to comprehend something more about fear as we reflect on the fear felt by God's chosen people of old and for many sojourners during biblical times. People who carried out God's plan oftentimes when feeling afraid. Take again for example David. Described as a mighty man of valor and a warrior and recognized as the Lord being with him, running from King Saul he strode into enemy territory feigning to have lost all capacity to think rationally after having become so afraid of King Saul who tried repeatedly to take his life. But this did not stop God from anointing David as king over Israel even before he ran. And Gideon and Joshua too were afraid and like David, both are described as courageous warriors. Moses, Jehoshaphat, Jacob, Elijah, and Peter in the New Testament and a host of others felt fear so I believe we can acknowledge that God calls ordinary people to do extraordinary feats despite suffering bouts of fear. God chooses those with shaky knees and all because He knows those who will move forward despite feeling fear while they are being developed into the person God knows they can become. We acknowledge our fear but we trust our God. This characterizes most of those God used in the Bible, and even those He uses today.

God is amazing! I didn't plan to write this story you are reading and neither did I plan to write the previous story you just read, but both narratives seem to connect together. Hours before writing either story while still lying in bed, the thought came to me to add two more engaging life experiences before ending this chapter. *But about what? And where should they be placed?* were the thoughts and questions running through my mind. Then seemingly out of nowhere, God stirred my spirit when He gave me the titles *No Fear?* and *In The Midst Of It All* and then again when He gave me the insight on where these two stories would perfectly fit. With my spirit aroused, I arose quickly and headed straight to my computer and just like that, out came both stories which share something we all need to hear as we walk out our journey with God. In doubting and fearful moments, God has already gone before us and planned the road ahead. He knows our thoughts before we encounter such places and decidedly, He knows just what to do to keep us grounded in enough faith and conviction to continue moving forward. To me, this is the epitome of having courage. Perhaps God had me write this particular story to encourage others to confront their crippling thoughts by remembering to call upon Him in an hour of need which demonstrates the faith needed to awaken the strength and fortitude to move forward in order to prevail. Acknowledging the presence of fear inevitably can be contrary to what some may think leads me to ponder if this is a reason the word *fear* is mentioned so many times in the Bible. Although when fear is mentioned in the Bible, it relates to different situations, in the New King James Version, fear is mentioned 457 times, and fear is mentioned 383 times in the New American Standard Bible and roughly the same number of times it appears in the New American Standard Bible (1995). When referring to man's natural fear of something which is mentioned frequently in the Bible, overcoming fear must be something many struggle with. I love reflecting on God's comforting words when He proclaims, "Do not fear, for I am with you; do not anxiously look about you, for I am your God. I will strengthen you, surely I will help you, surely I will uphold you with My righteous right hand."[24] But because people of faith can struggle with fear, God calls on us to be courageous just as he did with Joshua. Courage, I have come to understand is having the faith and the conviction to move forward despite feeling fear.

Recently, I met a woman who said she had no fear of anything. *That must be wonderful*, I thought to myself, but not realistic. Having no desire to entertain indulging in fear or to promote it, I believe she is wrong, and God is right. Too many Bible stories written about ordinary people facing trembling circumstances and being transformed into valiant men and

---

24. Isaiah 41:10. (NASB95).

women of God. Too many past historic and current moments that speak to feeling fearful about something and achieving greatness in spite of it. God protects and provides for His people when things appear larger than life. Though wisdom is to be applied when facing fearful moments, sometimes there still remains casualties of war as a result of mankind's ill behaviors that continue to impact the world today. But the truth remains, it is God who determines the length, the depth, and the breath of each life. The consequences for actions and the judgment which follows also remain in His control.

Weeks after thinking I had completed this story, wouldn't you know God gave me a bit more to add. As I said in the beginning of this book, one thing that comes to mind in understanding something about knowing God is He continues to teach me things I did not know before.

A few days ago, I happen to say to someone I thought I could share some of my deepest thoughts with that something felt scary to me and right away I was hit over the head with Scripture. No words of comfort were spoken, no voice of concern aired so I perceived a religious spirit was operating. When someone shares openly from the heart, we just might need to be reminded the Word of God makes it very clear that as we have been comforted, we are to comfort others. His word makes known with lovingkindness He has drawn us to Himself. So while sharing our most intimate feelings, the space should be safe to do so especially with a brother or sister in the Lord. It is amazing to me the very next day while adding this experience to what I thought would complete my story, unexpectedly God opened my ears at just the right moment to hear a prominent pastor repeatedly mention different situations he described as "scary" to him and not a single person in the sanctuary or online commented negatively about his heartfelt assertion. But God did not stop there. One day after hearing this well-known pastor repeatedly mention situations he described as scary, I happen to receive an online message from In Touch Ministries titled, The Power of Prayer. This message stated, "When scary challenges come, ask your heavenly Father for help."[25] In times of feeling less than our best, we should be able to be open and honest with each other and admit how we feel because what we feel matters to God and so it should matter to those we know. But God did not stop here either. Late one night a few days later, a message about a sermon spoken by the late Pastor Stephen Darby all of

---

25. In Touch Ministries (online article). Inspired by The Teachings of Charles F. Stanley. "The Power of Prayer." November 14, 2024. 12:00 AM EST.

Growing Pains

a sudden popped up on my iPhone titled, It's In The Family. And what did Pastor Stephen Darby mention 11 years ago but a situation he described as "scary."[26] I am thankful God sent these three messages to me at these three different times not only to comfort and speak truth to my heart but to speak a word to the hearts of those who are reading this story. I am thankful God has gone beyond what I understood and heard to now add a deeper meaning to a message we all need to hear—prayer and dependence upon God is key when facing fear. Calling upon God in fearful moments is demonstrating active faith. So having the courage to move forward in challenging moments is not always done without the absence of fear. As mentioned earlier, courage is moving forward despite the presence of fear. God sees a heart that trembles, and He chooses to use this person anyway as we see reflected in life stories throughout the Bible.

Not all of our growing pains look the same. Many of us will come face to face with issues somebody else might not entertain at all. Would not have brought themselves into that space. But thank God for His amazing power and His compassionate grace and lovingkindness which brings us safely to the other side of whatever we're facing. Even when feeling fearful.

Heavenly Father, I thank You for always leading Your people in every situation and in moments of doubt and despair. Thank You for empowering arms of clay to extend to those who still need to know Your name, even in the church. When speaking God's word, timing and delivery is everything. *Added Note.* Right before including my last few comments in this story and before saving them to my computer, I sat down to begin my morning Bible study and lo and behold, as soon as I opened my Bible, the Holy Spirit led me to intuitively read Ezekiel, Chapter 12, Verses 17 and 18. I must admit, I could scarcely believe what my eyes beheld. In these two verses of Scripture, I see something I never saw before when I read—"Moreover, the word of the Lord came to me saying, 'Son of man, eat your bread with trembling, and drink your water with quivering and anxiety.' " I don't know all God is saying here, but these expressed words tie directly to my story only moments ago I thought I had completed. Searching for understanding, according to my Bible footnotes, the Bible commentators explained, "By eating his meals in fear and trembling, Ezekiel warned the people of the coming captivity."[27] Perhaps God led me to this exact Scripture to understand that

---

26. Steven Darby Ministries (online sermon). *It's In The Family (Message).* April 22, 2013.

27. NASB95.

sometimes He will use fear to send a message. When we consider everything taking place in the world today, we see God allowing the world to be shaken through fearful and trembling winds of adversity both natural and manmade. I believe God is speaking to the church.

> 2 Corinthians 1:3–4. Praise be to the God and Father of our Lord Jesus Christ, the Father of compassion and the God of all comfort, 4. who comforts us in all our troubles, so that we can comfort those in any trouble with the comfort we ourselves receive from God. (NIV)

Chapter 2

An Uphill Climb

God Brought Us Through

Just think for a moment about the place God has brought you from. Was it a place of recovering from the loss of a relationship? Or were you dealing with a health issue or a shattered dream or maybe you were mourning behind the death of a loved one? When we are intimately acquainted with God, we find that He is our bridge over troubled water. We find rest in His Word that proclaims He is near to the brokenhearted and saves those who are crushed in spirit.[1]

At some point in life, all of us have left something or someone behind, and God brought us through the pain of suffering loss as He renewed our strength to move beyond any unresolved residue left behind suffering from a tragedy we faced. Loss is hard and rising again into a healthy space can be a challenge. We can still hurt but yet rise again because the Spirit of God guides us and sets us free as we yield ourselves to Him. I have discovered that hardships build our faith and our trust in God. They serve a purpose that sometimes we don't readily see. Along the journey of healing, God refocuses our thoughts to remember things we can still be thankful for. Something we are called to remember are those we still have in our lives as we cherish old memories shared with those no longer with us. Along the way, God will open doors to embrace something new to refresh our spirit. Perhaps it may be a different way of viewing a past situation which sets

---

1. Psalm 34:18 (NASB95).

us free. Or sometimes just maybe in the amidst of our pain, God brings someone unexpectedly across our path to reveal that He has you and me in mind. He opens doors to opportunities to address moments of loneliness to encourage us that we are never forgotten. Although the uphill climb can meet with many unanticipated challenges, God continues to restore hope one step at a time. Hope that allows us to rest assuredly He will perfect that which concerns you and me.

In stressful and troubling seasons, recognizing that God remains our anchor can offer us the assurance we need to realize that we are never truly alone. Recalling that His only begotten Son often walked the earth alone, and remembering that He suffered loss, betrayal, rejection and the feeling of being separated from His heavenly Father as He hung on the cross while God watched over Him can provide us with the assurance of His presence. Calling to mind that God always provided for His Son's every need reassures us that God deeply cares for those He loves and for anyone suffering. Surely we can recognize through the life Christ lived God is acutely acquainted with every form of agony we might endure. When I think about Christ's suffering, it helps me to put things in a better perspective, and it helps me to recognize that nothing we will ever endure will change the way God sees us as His people whole and precious in His sight. As noted earlier, seeing yourself as whole can sometimes be a challenge. But taking hold of the truth that God lovingly fashioned whole people created in His image from the beginning of time can help shape the view we hold of ourselves.

The words I just expressed takes me back to something I recently shared with one of my nephews. While discussing the subject of marriage, I told him no such thing as two halves becoming whole as we had been told years ago because wholeness is what qualifies the connection between a husband and wife. Whole people coming together in marriage enables the marriage to work best. If one of the two does not see themselves as whole, the relationship can suffer from things that could have been avoided. It is only the hand of God that can take two whole people and knit them together as one.

Spiritual wellness is embedded in our purpose in order to live life with an overcoming spirit. And it is needed to succeed in places we've never been to before. God's plan for a life takes into account developing the endurance and insight necessary for each individual person to walk this journey unencumbered from a past of pain or regret to realize when we mess up, He gives second chances. Everything we go through has already been weighed in the hands of God and weaved into purpose to awaken a God response not only in the us but in the lives of those who are listening and willing to obey. God comes again to bring forth the times needed to build testimonies in our story to reveal His glory.

But consider that sometimes the very thing we come against is straight from the hand of the enemy. Though at the same time God allows it, He is working out His glory in our story. Consider His servant Job. Not only did God permit the enemy to buffet Job, even beforehand God had asked the enemy had he considered His servant Job. Surprisingly to me was learning that sometimes the very person we are confronting is meant to bring awareness to an issue that is not about us at all. Sometimes God is dealing with the change that needs to take place in another person's behavior by using you and me. What I have come to understand is sometimes when God is dealing with someone else's behavior by using you and me, unfortunately, most often they will turn the tables on you to make the issue all about you rather than looking within to change their behavior. But regardless of the situation we encounter, Satan's aim is to get us to focus on the mountain that needs to be moved rather than our God who moves the mountain. Only God can change someone's behavior so don't break yourself in trying to get someone to change. Keeping our eyes on the One who is the strength of our life builds unshakable faith to keep believing for something better no matter how strong the winds may blow. It is good to recognize that although we endure trials and heartache, the outcome of the battles we face has already been spiritually determined by our Lord and Savior when He died and rose from death to life. I have come to understand that our assignment determines the strength of the battles we face.

In speaking of enduring trials and heartache, deception is often a tool used by the enemy when we find ourselves faced with an unexpected and intense life issue. If you've ever been deceived, then you probably recognize by now who was standing behind the person who deceived you. Once you learn the lesson you are meant to understand, you no longer allow yourself to go through the same revolving door because you are sensitive to the spirit of deception when it is in the room. And you have come to realize that Satan can only suggest an idea or thought. He cannot bend the will. Keep in mind that deception may seem harmless at the moment, but the results it brings are always devastating and costly. So choose wisely your calling over momentary comfort. Mentioning the spirit of deception brings to mind another tool the enemy uses which is fear. Fear of the unknown.

Fear of walking alone. Fear in believing whatever is standing against you is greater than you can handle. As already mentioned, we are never truly alone and by recognizing that we can do nothing apart from God is a powerful truth to keep in the forefront of our minds. Regardless of whether we are dealing with natural fear of something harmful which is normal or dealing with the fear of stepping into new and unchartered territory, God has already set a plan in motion for us to succeed though His plan often calls for courage and will always call for dependence upon Him. Consider Gideon in the Book of Judges. Gideon had to deal with disabling fear before walking out a God assignment:

> Now the same night it came about that the Lord said to him, "Arise, go down against the camp, for I have given it into your hands.
>
> But if you are afraid to go down, go with Purah your servant down to the camp, and you will hear what they say; and afterwards your hands will be strengthened that you may go down against the camp." So he went with Purah his servant down to the outposts of the army that was in the camp.
>
> Now the Midianites and the Amalekites and all the sons of the east were lying in the valley as numerous as locusts; and their camels were without number, as numerous as the sand on the seashore.
>
> When Gideon came, behold, a man was relating a dream to his friend. And he said, "Behold, I had a dream; a loaf of barley bread was tumbling into the camp of Midian, and it came to the tent and struck it so that it fell, and turned it upside down so that the tent lay flat."
>
> And his friend answered and said, "This is nothing less than the sword of Gideon the son of Joash, a man of Israel; God has given Midian and all the camp into his hand."
>
> And it came about when Gideon heard the account of the dream and its interpretation, that he bowed in worship. He returned to the camp of Israel and said, "Arise, for the Lord has given the camp of Midian into your hands."[2]

In any situation we face, God will always send the help we need even if the only help we need is simply to recognize we can stand alone with Him. In words of redeeming hope to uplift the spirit of man, the Lord declares, "Behold, I am the LORD, the God of all flesh; is anything too difficult for

---

2. Judges 7:9–15. (NASB95).

Me?"³ And again as proclaimed in the Book of Luke, "The things impossible with men are possible with God."⁴ When God makes a promise, He has the power to fulfill it.

From Gideon's life story we can take hold to believing that just as God was there for Gideon, He is here for us too. Whether God sends someone across your path to encourage your faith or He sends someone to work alongside you as He did with Gideon, or even if His plan is for you to walk the path alone, His invisible presence is always there. We need only believe.

Another tool the enemy uses is doubt. The enemy wastes no time in chasing after a word sown in the heart hoping that we question whether the word we received from God is true or not. Going all the way back to Eve in the Garden of Eden, we can see the enemy's tricks are not new. We can recognize the spirit posing the question, *Did God really say that?* which is exactly the situation that unfolded for me. Let me share it.

God gave me a dream while I was employed at a prominent bank. In my dream, I saw I would be leaving this company which I longed to do. Although the complete story is disclosed in a previous book, it brings to light something worth mentioning about God-given dreams.

When I had this dream, God made it known to me that I would be leaving my then present company. However, initially God didn't give me the exact time of my departure, but as the months passed by, one day, He did. Two years is the answer spoken to my heart that I understood God was saying to me while reading about someone else's life story recorded on the pages of the Bible. When I finally left this company, it turned out to be exactly two years just as I had read in someone else's life story written thousands of years ago. Something I have come to understand is before a storm ends, things often get worse before they get better. A few months before departing this company, I began to experience some of the bitterest trials I have ever experienced in life. Things around me turned and became so severe that I began to doubt the dream *and* the timing God had previously made known to me. It wasn't until the tail end of these bitter trials the events shown to me in my dream begin to play out right before my eyes. When I recognized the events of my dream unfolding, I became acutely aware of God's delivering power and became so amazed that despite my doubting Him, He rekindled my faith to believe and to recognize if He said it, it doesn't matter what it looks like. What He speaks will be done. I saw

---

3. Jeremiah 32:27 (NASB95).
4. Luke 18:27 (NASB95).

the events in my dream unfold beginning with me receiving a phone call at my desk from my manager asking me to meet with him. Everything happened just the way I saw it in my dream right down to the day I departed this company. For me, this story brings to light another well-known truth—Before God brings us out of whatever situation we are experiencing, our faith will be severely tested. I believe this is how we get the word *testimony* in our story.

But unlike what took place in this story, there has been other times when God spoke to my heart about something forthcoming when He did not provide any definite time for things to materialize. One such time was about two years ago on 6/15/22.

On 6/15/22, I prayed for God to open a door to a better job opportunity for a loved one who was enduring immense trials at work over a prolonged period of time. While praying, God spoke to my heart about a new job for my loved one, but the only word He used to convey a timing was the word "soon." Do I ever see so clearly now that God's timing for something *soon* to take place is solely His own because three months shy of two years had passed by before God spoke to my heart again about my loved one's new job opportunity coming into fruition. This second time God spoke to my heart, I didn't connect the dots because almost two years had passed by. So three months prior to God answering my prayer request of two years ago, I heard God speak to me to get ready to hear good news from my loved one. The good news I received turned out to be news about a new job opportunity just as God had spoken to me almost two years earlier. Now I understood God had come to inform me three months ahead of time that good news was forthcoming from my loved one. All I could do was cry tears of joy and to thank God profusely when my loved one shared the good news about a promising job opportunity. Something I can rest with is knowing that God is a promise keeper, but an area I've found which sometimes needs refreshing is reminding myself during a waiting season God's timing often takes longer than we think. If Father Abraham was alive today, I feel certain he would agree.

In getting to understand something about knowing God, it takes the span of a lifetime. It takes examining our own life story to see where God has made Himself known in the midst of our own self will. It takes connecting with biblical passages and specific Scriptures that God has led us to as it relates to our specific needs and life events. It involves listening to testimonies from others, sharing with others, and from hearing God's voice calling out to hearts and ears attuned to His Spirit. It takes discernment too. And it takes applying wisdom and growing in knowledge and understanding. It takes having a personal relationship with the God who created it all. From my life stories, by now you probably notice I am a serious note taker when it comes to tracking my journey with God. Though I could go on and on about God's amazing exploits that I witnessed, what book could hold it all because His glorious deeds just keep coming.

Before I close this story, there is another point worth mentioning which stands out to me in understanding aspects about God I had not known before—our relationship with God is foremost in successfully achieving goals that call out His name because as believers in Christ everything we accomplish in His name carries His fragrance so others will know we've been in His presence. Imperative to learning something more about knowing God is being adequately grounded in His Word. Speaking what we've learned from studying the Bible and continuing to grow in a deeper understanding of His Word, His Spirit and His intervention in our lives and staying prayerful will all make a difference to those we minister to so they too will desire to know the God of the Bible and the power of prayer. As rightly stated, "Where the word of the Lord is, there is power."[5]

As we climb our mountains and move forward in life, may we hold on to the unshakable faith to believe that God has an appointed time to take us from where we once were to the place we need to be in order to fulfill our destiny if not already living it.

> I Peter 4:12–13. Beloved, do not be surprised at the fiery ordeal among you, which comes upon you for your testing, as though some strange thing were happening to you; 13. but to the degree that you share the sufferings of Christ, keep on rejoicing; so that also at the revelation of His glory, you may rejoice with exultation. (NASB95)

---

5. Reverend, Doctor, Military Colonel James D. Keys. In-house sermon, *Here Today, Gone Tomorrow*. 03/23/2025.

Something About Knowing God

Dressing In The Full Armor of God

As the Word of God declares we war not against flesh and blood, but against principalities and darkness in high places. We are in spiritual warfare. And His Word provides us clear instruction on how to dress in the full armor of God to stand in defense against the enemy of our soul who prowls around like a roaring lion seeking whom he may devour. As we confront trials which are an inevitable part of life, the outcomes will attest to our faith and our trust in God and if paying attention, we will understand His purpose for allowing the trial. The outcome will also reveal the path we have chosen to follow whether it is one of leaning on God or leaning on something or someone else to get us through the trial.

The Word of God makes known to us the enemy comes to steal, kill and destroy. Thanks be to the God of all grace the enemy can only *seek* to devour and not *will* devour us. God's Word sets us free in heart and spirit to walk His path of victory! By understanding the enemy is not the flesh and blood we see standing in front of us can temper our reaction to those who don't mind or are unaware of being used by the enemy. Applying this truth extends the choice to remain silent without the need to defend, explain, or validate ourselves to someone who either doesn't have our best interest at heart or won't hear us anyway. Sometimes an eye opener is the realization that everybody in our lives don't always belong for every season going forward in life. Especially when our emotional energy is consistently being drained behind repeatedly encountering harmful behaviors or toxic remarks. When this occurs, it is time for change. It is time to build healthy boundaries to safeguard your peace, to come out from among them and to be separate. It is time to choose you and to heal. Another point to make about the enemy of our soul is he wastes no time in observing us to strategically bait us when it comes to our likes and dislikes, our habits and any triggers or impulses we have including core values that we hold dearly. The enemy watches for moments of vulnerability, but remember he can only suggest an action or a thought to consider because he cannot control our will. Just as Jesus rebuked the enemy, we should follow in His footsteps, even if done silently under our breath. We win when we respond with God's Word of Truth, our strongest weapon.

Thinking about how the enemy studies our ways in trying to set us up to fall, remember when he came to Jesus three times to try to ensnare Him? The first time the enemy tried tempting Jesus to eat food based on

Jesus's need for provision rather than Jesus continuing to rely on His Father. Jesus had gone 40 days and 40 nights without food so the enemy knew His human body was in a position where some care could be readily provided. Being unsuccessful, the devil then tried to persuade Jesus to misuse His power to draw attention to Himself to prove He is who He is—the Messiah. When this attempt failed, the enemy tried a third time to entice Jesus with riches and by offering Him a different plan for His life. This reminds me of how important it is to observe behaviors the first time when meeting someone new with a smiling face who has not yet proven genuineness of heart. Remember the eyes are the window to the soul and they speak volumes. Besides, trust should be earned and not simply given to someone you barely know. It becomes a decision-making moment when sensing even a slight disturbance in your spirit and in moments when you don't understand why you are sensing something is off. You sense something is off because it is off. When not sure of a situation we are facing, we should ask ourselves, "What would Jesus do?" Remember, saying *yes* to the enemy is saying *no* to God.

When we dress in the full armor of God, we are instructed to stand in defense against the schemes of the devil which I believe indicates we are not to advance towards him in battle nor turn our backs to him either. We are to firmly stand our ground. The Bible also makes it very clear who our real enemy is by stating, "For our struggle is not against flesh and blood, but against the rulers, against the powers, against the world forces of this darkness, against the spiritual forces of wickedness in the heavenly places."[6] So when we face a spirit emanating from a heart of flesh that displays conduct in opposition to the character of God, we know who is standing behind the person we are facing and we should make the decision in this moment to turn away from the very appearance of evil. But sometimes, we can get caught up in the moment, and you may find yourself going through the same thing I did some years ago. This experience I am about to share, I find, is not new.

On June 30, 1989, I went camping with a family I felt close to and was caught off guard and not at all prepared to see the face of the enemy behind the face of my friend. While the mother and I sat together inside one of the tents, unexpectedly she began speaking in an unfriendly and quite hostile tone about an issue over money. All I could think about as I listened to her heated comments were the situations that unfolded before leaving on our camping trip. Whenever a remark was made about a purchase (and they

---

6. Ephesians 6:12. (NASB95).

insisted on doing all the shopping on the military base), I made sure to contribute. In fact, on a couple of occasions, I was told not to bother contributing at all because there would be enough provision for all of us. Needless to say, I felt humbled by my friend's remarks and in that moment, I only saw her face and not the face of enemy. After she vented, I offered additional funds which she accepted. After arriving home, I sought God's counsel for a second time because I surely prayed to Him while out camping. Nudged in my spirit this second time I prayed, I was led to read Psalm 66, Verse 10 through 12. While carefully examining the text I read, I could readily identify with the words written here because they spoke of being tried and refined as silver and going through fire. I was relieved when at the very end of Verse 12, it spoke of hope when mentioning God is bringing us into a place of abundance. Am I ever thankful that destructive storms don't last forever and thankful the armor of God fully protects us at times even when we don't even realize it. Without me uttering a word of defense, a short time later this friend reached out to me to apologize and our relationship continued. If not careful, Satan will use money to break up relationships, especially amongst family. Now back to dressing in the full armor of God.

The Book of Ephesians Chapters 4 and 5 explains to us how to walk wisely. In Chapter 6, we are told to stand strong in the Lord to overcome any resistance posed by the enemy and this chapter also explains how we are to dress in the full armor of God to enable us to stand firmly in defense. Also noted in Chapter 6 is a reminder to remain prayerful which is crucial to our walk of faith and in recognizing the voice of God. Beginning with Verse 13 of Chapter 6, in using God's weaponry when dressing in the full armor of God we are told to gird our loins with truth and to arm ourselves with the breastplate of righteousness. These pieces of armor I have come to understand are to prepare us to follow Christ by responding with integrity and faithfulness.[7] This armor guards our hearts to keep us in right standing with God while protecting us against any assaults of the enemy. Our feet shod with The Preparation of The Gospel of Peace is spiritual readiness to face the enemy which is produced by the good news of the Gospel of Peace.[8] The shield of faith extinguishes every flaming arrow the evil one sends as we stand in resolute faith in the Lord our God. If the enemy was

---

7. The Bible Knowledge Commentary. New Testament edition. John F. Walvoord & Roy B. Zuck. 1983.

8. The Bible Knowledge Commentary. New Testament edition. John F. Walvoord & Roy B. Zuck. 1983.

not going to attack us, we wouldn't need the shield. Now the last two pieces of armor are the helmet of salvation, which serves as God's protection for our minds, our thoughts against anything set against us, and the sword of the Spirit which is the only defensive weapon we use to combat all attacks from the enemy. The sword of the Spirit is the Word of God.

While re-reading this story, I reflected back on a recent experience I just had and I thought to myself, *Boy was I ever put to the test by the very words I had just written in my story.* This recent experience reminds me again that everything we say and everything we write is meant to be regarded by us first. Thanks to the Spirit of God, when recently attacked by the enemy through someone I thought I knew, I was able to weather the storm. Other than saying, "You didn't have to mock me like that," I remained silent. The enemy *is* a lie! After rethinking this experience, the thought weighing heavily on my heart was it is a terrible thing to be used by the enemy and not realize it. I don't think she saw herself being used by the enemy because she kept repeating unfiltered words in a small window of time. It is only by keeping close to our heart the choice to see whether our character displays God's character shining or not shining through our own behaviors that we can see ourselves in order to keep from being used by the enemy of our soul. If we don't foresee the enemy's hand in his attempts to ensnare us, then surely after voicing something disfavorable or yielding to fleshly conduct, we should be so bothered in our spirit that our heart is pricked to self-reflect. Seems to me not a lot of self-reflection is taking place in the world today. What do you think?

Within moments of concluding my story only God could have led me to read Isaiah, Chapter 11, Verse 5 where it speaks about the armor given to Christ while He walked the earth. Amazed by the words in this verse, to me, they seem to speak to our own armor of God as Verse 5 declares, "Also righteousness will be the belt about His loins, and faithfulness the belt about His waist."[9] Everything Christ accomplished was done in a spirit of righteousness and fairness which are attributes we should strive to follow.

In wielding our weaponry as we are dressed in the full armor of God, the Bible again provides clear instruction in its use when stating, "For the weapons of our warfare are not carnal but mighty in God for pulling down strongholds, casting down arguments and every high thing that exalts itself against the knowledge of God, bringing every thought into captivity to the

---

9. NASB95.

obedience of Christ."[10] Truly the Word of God sets us free! Quoting words I recently heard spoken by a well-known pastor that I believe aptly describe our walk here on earth, "Christianity is a battlefield, not a playground."[11]

> Isaiah 54:17. No weapon formed against you shall prosper, and every tongue which rises against you in judgment You shall condemn. This is the heritage of the servants of the Lord, and their righteousness is from Me, says the Lord. (NKJV)

---

10. 2 Corinthians, Chapter 10, Verses 4–5. (NKJV).
11. Smokie Norful. Online sermon. *God is Able. He Did That.* 10/07/2024.

An Uphill Climb

From Shame to Glory!

The blood of Christ Jesus covers our shame. As declared in His Word, there is no condemnation for those who are in Christ Jesus. No one has to live with the shame of their past. You are never your condition. So detach yourself from defeating thoughts so you are able to rise in renewed hope and undisputed faith to see yourself the way God sees you as fearfully and wonderfully made. Following His precepts carry the fragrance of His glory in your life story. Jesus came to set the captives free! The Bible will unshackle what may have been hidden treasures inside you as you walk with the God who created it all. As we grow in our understanding and in our faith, we come to believe and ready ourselves to receive His lovingkindness when we align ourselves with the truth of the Bible as it proclaims, "The Lord's loving kindnesses indeed never cease, for His compassions never fail. They are new every morning; great is Thy faithfulness."[12] Call to mind the woman at the well whose story is found in the Book of John, Chapter Four. Because of her story, many came to seek out Christ. This is the same woman who lived a past that was less than desirable.

I have come to realize that our failures can serve as stepping stones to our spiritual development. I've also come to understand that God will fix the hinge on the door of someone's life that has been broken. It is never too late for God to build His story inside your story. Consider the age of Moses when he was called by God. Moses was 80 years old and his brother Aaron was 83. So age doesn't matter when it comes to fulfilling a God-given assignment. All God-given dreams and inspirations are meant to be birthed, not buried. So don't allow Satan to silence your divinely-given dreams and inspirations. We are meant to reign with our King! Our value is not up for negotiation.

Thinking again of Moses and also of God's servant David, no matter their former shame, Moses led God's people out of bondage and David was crowned king over Israel despite his spotted past. We are to put on the garment of praise for a spirit of heaviness and to rise in faith to believe that we can achieve the high calling we have in Christ Jesus. We rise from shame to glory when we receive God's word of hope spoken to our hearts. Words such as those we find in Psalm 126 assure us, "Those who sow in tears shall reap with joyful shouting."[13] And words of hope are also written in the

---

12. Lamentations 3:22, 23. (NASB95).
13. Verse 5. NASB95.

Book of Hebrews, Chapter Eleven and in First Peter Chapter One. Taking God's word to heart will heal broken places when we are able to believe that our former troubles are forgotten because they are hidden from His sight.[14] Trusting in God's word lifts the spirit of man and assures us of our rightful place in Him.

Our God changes not. As He called forth many people in the Bible who lived before us with a past riddled in shame, God remains the same today, yesterday, and forevermore. So lift your head in renewed faith to know that you are a treasure as you read and remember the life stories written on the pages of the Bible that tell of God using people mightily who had a tattered past. When we place our faith and trust in God, our past cannot stop us. And our deepest scars can be healed. Tarnished vessels God uses for His glory are not only revealed in the Old Testament but are also clearly shown in the New Testament. Call to mind the life of Peter. Not only did Peter deny knowing His Savior, he even cursed and swore he did not know Him. Yet Peter was a chosen vessel who went on to proclaim the message of God's Son. Peter was also a chosen foundational leader within the church. There is purpose with your name on it so let not your heart remain troubled. We rise from shame to glory!

We never know what God has in store unless He reveals it so it is worth walking with Him. In God's hand, nothing in life is wasted. When we give everything we have over to God, we can expect something better because God transforms us into instruments of praise to tell others His story.

> Isaiah 60:1. Arise [from the depression and prostration in which circumstances have kept you—rise to a new life]! Shine (be radiant with the glory of the Lord), for your light has come, and the glory of the Lord has risen upon you! (AMP)

---

14. Isaiah 65:16b. (NASB95).

An Uphill Climb

God Has Something Better

I believe we can all agree we desire the best to unfold in life. The best for ourselves and the best for those we love. But sometimes in order to live out our best life, it may create the need to change something about our thinking or something about our lifestyle pattern. Maybe we need to change the way we see ourselves if what we see does not align with the view God holds of us as spoken about in the Bible. We may need to change something about a behavior when deep inside our heart we know a certain thing we are doing does not line up with the character of God. Just because something feels comfortable does not mean it is the right thing to do. We will find that whatever we feed on emotionally and socially shapes our character. If we really think about it, we can recognize we will attract the spirit in others when that same spirit is operating in us. When we desire something better to unfold in life, we must choose better because God has something better. When we consider the consequences of actions or words spoken to others and words spoken over our own lives, we become more conscious of situations drawn to us not visible to an unseeing eye. We stop making excuses for comfortable albeit undeserving behaviors. Guided by the truth of God's Word, though spoken long ago, it guides us today when it declares, "Let us examine and probe our ways, and let us return to the Lord."[15]

As said before, Satan comes to steal, kill, and destroy and he wants nothing more than to destroy a life or to keep a life in spiritual bondage to old cycles of behaviors that aren't freeing. Age doesn't matter either. And neither does being saved nor unsaved when it comes to behaviors that stunt spiritual and personal growth. All the more reason to pray fervently and to seek outside help when it is needed. Especially the need to seek godly counsel when dealing with behaviors, addictions and impulses that can only lead to a life of regret. When our inner peace repeatedly unravels and brings us back to the same place again and again, we know we are dealing with a momentary pleasure. And we also know the enemy is involved. Consider now what you might lose behind indulging in pleasures that rule against godly principles and you will find it is not worth the cost you may pay in the end.

In overcoming ungodly behaviors, it not only involves unpacking negative feelings in the ears of man whether to a counselor, a therapist, a pastor or a close friend, but overcoming costly negative behaviors involves

---

15. Lamentations 3:40. (NASB95).

Something About Knowing God

the ears and the heart of God. In fact, God is the One we should go to first, but often we don't. I say this because He created us so He can handle whatever is working against us. And besides, He already knows what we're thinking because nothing is hidden from His sight. No matter what you're facing, disengage from any hidden disappointment you have in your heart that can cancel your faith to believe for something better. God is rooting for you and it is a good time to root for yourself too. The bottom line is there is nothing that can stop God's plan from bearing fruit in a life yielded to Him. I believe this also includes those striving earnestly to know His name.

As yielded vessels of Christ we know we can't reach everybody. And we look to the Word of God to recall that some of us water, some plant, but it is God who gives the increase. In Matthew Chapter 13, Jesus explains the Parable of the Sower. The Lord makes known that some seed falls on a path where the enemy comes immediately to take away the word sown in the heart and some seed falls on rocky ground where there is no depth so the hearer of the word falls away. Some seed as Jesus stated is sown amongst thorns where the cares of this world enter in to choke out the word sown in the heart. But then there is the seed sown on good soil and these are the ones who receive the Word of God with gladness and produce an abundance of fruit.

The Bible warns us to test the spirit to see whether it is of God.[16] Surely had our eyes been open we would have made a few different choices earlier in life. This may sound a bit whimsical, but recently, I mentioned to my oldest grandson that we can learn life lessons from songs of the past. For instance, take the old song Smiling Faces sung by The Undisputed Truth. This song tells the truth that smiling faces sometimes tell lies, a lesson many of us have learned the hard way. And what about another old song that speaks of wisdom when relating to a story of an old woman who befriended a sick snake she saw laying on the ground. Because of the snake's pleading, the old woman picked up the snake and took it home to nurse it back to health. But from the very beginning, undoubtedly this snake noticed the old woman's unguarded and caring spirit because it affectionately addressed her as "tender woman." Against better judgement this old woman took the snake home and nursed it back to health only to be bitten in the end by a poisonous snake that wasted no time in telling her, "You knew I was a snake before you took me in." There is a lot of wisdom in this old song. Forming relationships unguarded without healthy boundaries in place or not giving

---

16. I John 4:1.

An Uphill Climb

a relationship the time needed to disclose true character causes one to live with regrets. When a person heals, they set boundaries which are often misunderstood as walls to keep others out. You learn to protect your inner peace.

We are to remain vigilant no matter how small a matter is when it disturbs our inner peace. We are to follow the unction of the Holy Spirit at all times which keeps us safe. Although you may not be able to put your finger on a specific problem, you can sense something is off. This is the Holy Spirit alerting you not to move forward.

This reminds me of the time years ago about a situation that unfolded while in the process of selling my two-story home. I had told myself that I wanted to move in three months which would have been in the month of October. One day, I picked up the newspaper to look at rental properties and just so happened to see a listing for two properties owned by the same man. And wouldn't you know, one of the properties would become available in the month of October. After scheduling an appointment to see the property scheduled to be ready in October, the owner wanted me to look at the available property first. As a carpenter, I am sure he felt proud of his work. When we arrived at this property, the first thing that caught my attention was the street where the property was located. It did not feel like home to me. And when I stepped inside the house, again, it did not feel like home. When we drove to the second property, although at the time it was definitely a disaster on the inside with floors and walls needing to be redone, I saw potential, and I felt peace. Stepping out on the sidewalk felt just like home to me so I choose this one. The owner could not understand why I would choose sometime that was broken, instead of a home that was move-in ready. Aside from the date of me wanting to move, the appearance of the homes had nothing to do with my decision. It was witnessing the peace in my spirit as I followed the Holy Spirit's lead. This readily reminds me of the time I purchased my very first home. As soon as my friend Brenda and I crossed over the threshold, we both looked at each other and exclaimed with broad smiles, "This is it!" Both of us felt the peace of the Holy Spirit at the exact same moment. This home too proved to be a blessing. And it had an interesting beginning.

When I first saw this home, back then I communicated to the real estate company that I wanted to purchase it. Then reality hit me—I didn't have enough money for the downpayment. So I called the real estate company again and told them that I wouldn't be purchasing this home. About three days later, it dawned on me—*they said I could save while waiting on the home to close*. They had told me it would take several months to close because of conditions the owners were facing. When I called them again, not only had the home not sold, in unison they told me, "We knew this home was for you!" We all laughed and so over the course of several months, I would go to water and feed the flowers in the front yard and tend to any weeds. Though the owners had moved out of the state, they had arranged for the grass to be cut. One day while there, a next door neighbor walked across the lawn and joined me in the front yard. He looked at me and said, "You got the house yet? I see you coming over here taking care of the yard." I told him, "No," that I had not been approved yet to purchase this home. But in my heart, I knew this would be my home. On another day after finding out I had been approved, after joining me in the yard, this same neighbor pointed at me and said, "I knew that a woman was going to buy this home." The house was painted yellow.

It pays to follow the unction of the Holy Spirit no matter what it looks like. And if paying attention, we can glean wisdom from simple things in life that lead to a better experience unfolding before us.

As you discard old clothes in your closet or old possessions you no longer desire to keep around your home, take a spiritual checkup on things that trouble your spirit or anything that doesn't contribute to you living a principled life and get rid of it. We don't wait until we feel like changing our direction when our direction needs to change.

Something else to keep in mind as you travel through life—we train people how to treat us so pay attention to how you are allowing yourself to be handled. Take hold to believing that since God is for us, we can find rest in knowing that He has something better in mind. We can rest in His affirming words as recorded in Psalm 31, Verse 19 which proclaims, "He has stored up goodness for those who take refuge in Him." This is where I strive daily to live. How about you?

> 1 Peter 2:9. But you are a chosen generation, a royal priesthood, a holy nation, His own special people, that you may proclaim the praises of Him who called you out of darkness into His marvelous light; (NKJV)

An Uphill Climb
Building A New Foundation

Here's another question for you. What do you do when you desire something new in place of something you discarded or no longer find useful or when you desire to build new memories? There is one thing I hope you have discovered by reading the stories in this book— how vital it is to follow after God's heart to successfully move forward in life. I hope this next truth resonates with both of us—God transforms hearts of clay so that we don't always remain the same. As we grow in Christ Jesus, as we take on new challenges, and while walking through new doors of opportunities, hopefully we find that we are growing in wisdom and understanding and knowledge about the purpose and will of God. And hopefully, as we learn we allow the quietness of heart and confidence in God to be our strength.[17]

God builds our foundation. And as our master builder, He doesn't build a life based on yesterdays, and neither does He build a life based on who might have left. I've learned that God will dismiss people from your life because they are not meant to be a part of His plan currently unfolding. As the master builder of our foundation, God calls us to depend solely upon Him rather than on the person who might have left or upon any *one* person who happens to be in your life now. Although we do support one another. God has built us for connection, but we depend on Him. There are other times when someone leaves without saying a word for reasons unknown to you so you don't know how to fix the problem. But then sometimes someone close to you becomes silent which causes the relationship to diminish. I've come to understand in this situation, a person may choose to become silent because perhaps they are dealing with a traumatic health or personal life issue so they may choose to remain to themselves. But just maybe you are dealing with a relationship like the one I faced not too long ago.

Some years ago before beginning to work on this book, I suggested to an old friend we should write a book together. Initially, my first thought was to write this book as a solo project, but because of years of spending time together, I thought to include her too. As soon as we agreed to write a book together, I felt a twinge of unrest in my spirit, but didn't know why. It turns out a few years later before we could even began working on writing this book, our relationship ended. Several months later, God stirred my heart to start working on the book you are now reading. I understand now this book was meant to be a solo project which must be the reason I felt a

---

17. Isaiah 30:15.

disturbance in my spirit when we agreed to write this book together. Taking the time to reflect on our relationship, I pondered questionable moments spent together. One time in particular stood out to me. It was at the time I wrote a previous book. She had agreed to help me within two weeks with something related to the book's finish. But after three months had passed by, one day I mentioned to her that she told me she would help me in two weeks but three months had gone by. In a fiery tone she remarked, "Maybe I'm not the friend you need to do this! Maybe you need to get another one of your friends to do it!" Her words caused me to pause and to question the soundness of our relationship, and also to wonder *where did these words come from?* A little later thank God, she changed her mind. But then came the time when out of nowhere in an accusatory tone she blurted out, "God isn't doing the same thing for me He's doing for you!" as though I had something to do with God's designed purpose for my life and for her life. Taken totally off guard, the only thing that came to my mind was to try to reassure her God has given her gifts and talents too. In the aftermath of reflecting on moments like these, I have come to painfully realize our love for others will sometimes blind us to seeing what is right in front of us. I've come to understand that someone you think of as a friend can see the treasure God has placed inside you, but you may have a hard time recognizing what's truly living on the inside of them. And I've come to realize everybody can't handle what God has placed in your life. Lesson learned. If God is not there in that moment of time, things won't change. Something else I've come to understand is God leads us purposefully even when we don't know it. But He knows the precise time to awaken slumbering eyes. A comment made by this same old friend who I now believe was meant to affirm my calling to write books when I didn't even see it took place on the day when again, out of the blue she remarked, "Vera, you are a writer. Not me." God has opened my eyes to see that sometimes people come into our lives for only a season or a reason, and at other times they are to be treasured for a lifetime. Even in lifetime relationships there can be unanticipated separations for a season. As Pastor Tony Evans pointedly remarked, "Sometimes you try to bring people where they don't belong."

If we desire the best plan to unfold, if we want the best laid foundation, then we must strive to follow after God's own heart with all of our heart, soul, and mind. And when we mess up, we fess up. I have also come to understand not to base my plans totally on things I may know at the moment because God brings new insight alongside things I already know.

I've discovered when there is a call on your life, God will separate you from the crowd and sometimes from someone you once thought of as a friend. Sometimes walking in solitude is not our choice, but it is a space of time God arranges to be with Him alone to drown out distractions, turmoil, and any drama so we are able to focus fully on the task He has equipped and called us to accomplish. Only purpose in mind is what I see because of the assignment He calls us to fulfill. But as we fulfill His call upon our lives, He doesn't leave out opportunities to share with others we meet along the way. Ministry is a call, and one that I have come to recognize as I once heard said is often a lonely one.

As we walk with God, the eye is opened to recognizing the difference between a true friend and a so-called friend and to recognize those who are only meant to be in our life for a season or for a reason. And we learn the truth behind what having a family really means. Learning this truth stops you from excusing behaviors that God doesn't excuse. When it comes to thoughts of a true friendship, I often think of the supportive relationship shared between David and Johnathan in the Old Testament. The outpouring of their regard for each other helps to paint a picture to discern true friendship from random acts of kindness amid insults. I often think about what the Bible says of the one who sticks closer than a brother, a relationship not often found but when it is found, it should be cherished. When it comes to peering through the eyes of God's love, if you have no problem repeatedly crushing someone else's spirit, you might want to consider where this spirit is coming from. I feel certain in this situation you have your own blemishes too with three fingers pointing back at you.

I love what God has revealed to me about His call upon my life. And I greatly value the undeniable outpouring of His love and the relationships I share amongst true friendships where there is no envy. I am also thankful for the embracing love shown by close family, if only a few, as I believe you do too. When it comes down to looking over my own life, "The Lord is my portion says my soul, therefore, I have hope in Him."[18] I honor my journey with God and His confirming words spoken to my heart many years ago written down on a small torn off piece of paper I keep taped to the front of my computer monitor. One day over 20 years ago while in prayer, God spoke something precious to my heart about my call to write. The words He spoke to my heart at that moment were too wonderful for me to embrace so every now and then, I glance at them as a reminder. But oh how we grow in

---

18. Lamentations 3:24. (NASB95).

developing insight about God that we might not have known before. And how beautiful it is to be refreshed in mind and spirit to embrace everything He makes known to us that is meant to be a part of His plan for our lives. Took me 20 years to fully embrace the words God spoke to my heart that day which brings to mind the roughly 20 years of preparation it took prior to David sitting on the throne and reigning as a king. Sometimes the preparation process can be a long one. The thing that happened which caused me to fully embrace God's words spoken to me came about one day while I was reading a familiar passage in the Bible. Suddenly my eyes became open to see something I had not taken note of before. Although I'd read these same words many times over the passing years, on this particular day I was able to comprehend God's intent behind words He had spoken to my heart 20 years earlier.

Everything we accomplish in life is not going to be received by everybody we care about. Even when considering the Bible, as life-sustaining and powerful as God's Word is, it is not received by everybody. So when God gives you a dream or an inspired goal or a certain pursuit to accomplish, do it for His glory and for no other reason. If He's called you to carry out a specific plan for your life, there is purpose wrapped up in it. As He gives voice to earthen vessels through word, song, and various forms of art, use it for His glory so others will come to know His story and will learn something imperative for living life in honor of God and in honor of His divine creativity. We are God's treasure hidden in clay pots and His voice deserves to be heard, foremost throughout the Bible, through His own creation and through the earthen vessels He chooses to speak through. Recently, I happened to hear someone say, "Hearing God's voice is the birthright of every true Believer."[19]

If we love what we do more than we love God, we've surely missed it. God first, our family and His people comes next. But this in no way means that God forgets about the one He sends with a message for others. He takes care of us as we take care of His business just as it happened for our Lord and Savior as He went about His Father's business. We are to esteem others more than we esteem ourselves. And what better way to live than to be kingdom builders.

If this message is for you, then believe that no matter what you've experienced in life or feel you could have done better, God chose you anyway. He knows exactly what is needed to build a solid foundation. Remember,

---

19. Captured from the Movie *Mountain Top*. 2017.

An Uphill Climb

He asks this question, "Is anything too difficult for Me?"[20] And the answer is a resounding, "No." What the enemy meant for evil, God turns it around for our good. God builds destiny out of shame, failure, and regret, and He uses His own delays as His perfect timing to work out His divine plan, especially for a life yielded to Him. God builds beauty from ashes, and He carries out His divine purpose despite mishaps and despite who may have left your life. As you walk with God, you will find Him to be the best father, the best friend, the best doctor, the best of everything you will ever have.

> I Corinthians 6:17. But the one who joins himself to the Lord is one spirit with Him. (NASB95)

> II Corinthians 1:21. But it is God Who confirms and makes us steadfast and establishes us [in joint fellowship] with you in Christ, and has consecrated and anointed us [enduing us with the gifts of the Holy Spirit]; (AMPC)

---

20. Jeremiah 32:27 (NASB95).

Something About Knowing God

Dancing in The Rain

Because we know who we are in Christ Jesus, we can dance in the rain when we rise to encourage our own spirit during stormy seasons of life following in the footsteps of David. After experiencing grave tragedy and after being greatly distressed, David encouraged his own spirit in the Lord. As noted in the Bible we read, "But David strengthened himself in the Lord his God."[21] We can choose hope instead of discouragement when we call to mind the battle belongs to the Lord and when we call to mind, when the Lord fights we win. Though at times, like David, we may stumble and fall, but we rise again when we remember that anything touching our lives had to first be sifted through God's hands. In earth shattering moments, we can choose to dance in the rain not because of what happened, but because we are still here. And this means we are blessed and we have something to be thankful for when we realize we didn't lose everything. Whether we praise God silently in heart or sing songs aloud, we are to encourage ourselves in the Lord our God. We dance in the rain despite the storm, despite fiery furnace experiences where I believe God is asking, "Will you trust Me?"

We are joint heirs with Christ Jesus and because God lives in us this is the best of anything and everything we could ever possess. As we walk out our journey with God, we can't afford to wait until the battle is over to praise His great name. We grow when we choose to focus on something greater than our current condition that cannot change for the better without Him. This brings to mind the story of Paul and Silas. Remember it was their praise in song to God that opened the doors of their prison cell. Praise is a weapon that turns the tide in our favor just as it did for them.

When we become consciously aware of dressing in spiritual battle garb, our stand becomes stronger. We recognize we are equipped with the best God has for us to safeguard our inner peace. We gird up our loins with the strength to stand against spiritual attacks launched against us as we begin to realize the way we carry ourselves in a storm tells where our confidence and faith lies. Although storms in life can bring turbulent weather conditions, sometimes a rainy season of storms comes to water a barren land. While some may be facing intense weather that seem to rend life apart, others may have been living in a dry and barren season where water is desperately needed to drench the dry places. To bring life to what was once a hopeful dream. Wherever we are in a rainy season, one thing is for

---

21. First Samuel 30:6. (NASB95).

sure. God remains intentional. When we witness storms in a rainy season that conflict with our own thoughts it leads me to ask God this question, "Lord what are You saying here?" One thing I know is when we praise God in stormy weather it silences the howling winds and it brings peace to our inner man. Praising God spreads wings of hope inside an ailing heart. I like what I read this morning in the Book of Job. Only God could have led me to something I would not have known when trying to understand the unexpected storm a friend was facing. In my Bible footnotes for the Book of Job Chapter 39:13-17, it states, ". . .just as behind the trials of the godly, which seem so unreasonable to Job, lies the wise purpose of God."[22] God is purposeful in everything He does. And there are times when I see myself here just as these words explain about Job's time of testing which is just the place my friend happened to be.

But despite the many hard places God has given entry into my life, I decided a long time ago to dance in the rain. Yes, I have cried out just like we all do at times, but I know to rise up in praise to His great name and to speak to the mountains be thou removed and cast into the sea. Thinking about praising God in turbulent weather takes me all the way back to the time God spoke to me about some of my past behaviors He associated with behaviors of His chosen people in biblical times while at the same moment, He gave me the spiritual name Judah as mentioned in an earlier story. But what I didn't say when I told this story is something I did not know until much later on. I came to understand a name change given by God signifies a change in relationship with Him. It also indicates character and it reveals something about the desire one has in serving God. The name Judah means praise. As my old friend who often compared my life to hers, one thing she pointed out about my life is that many times I would dance before God and thank Him for the smallest things. It took me many years to connect my dancing before the Lord matched the character He saw in me when He gave me the spiritual name Judah. Something else I now understand which is often seen in the Bible as declared by God, He gives His servants a new name.[23]

Am I ever grateful that God placed in my heart when my children were still quite young to start our prayer time by singing praise songs to Him. Am I am ever grateful that God used me to play a meaningful part in showing my sons when they young that praising God as we circled and

---

22. New American Standard Bible (1995).
23. Isaiah 65:15.

danced around our old coffee table seven times shifted our circumstances to open the door to something good for our future. I believe I fit the name Judah for I have learned to dance in the rain.

> Psalm 149:3. Let them praise His name with dancing; let them sing praises to Him with timbrel and lyre. (NASB95)
>
> Psalm 150:6. Let everything that has breath praise the LORD. Praise the LORD! (NASB95)

Added Note: When God revealed to me aspects about my past behaviors that He likened to behaviors of those who lived long ago, it seemed a bit unusual to me. But perhaps it isn't. Right before completing this book, God came through again with something unexpected that I did not know before. A close nephew of mine called me on the phone one day and without me sharing my own story, he told me his story. God had spoken to his heart about some of his behaviors too. My nephew said one day not long ago as he watched a televised sermon, he listened while a man of God shared how God had explained to him something about his behaviors, and in that very moment the man said he argued with God because he felt the things God was saying to him were not true at all. A short while later after hearing this man's sermon, my nephew said he heard God speak to his heart about a behavior he was doing that needed correcting. At first, my nephew said he argued with God too. My nephew told me he said to God, "That's not me! I'm glad I'm not like that!" But he found out he was just like God said he was. God is truly amazing! Twenty-five years later, I have learned it is not only me who God will humble and speak to the heart when revealing something about our personal behaviors and attitudes. I know now at least it has been this man of God my nephew spoke about and also my nephew himself. Before getting off the phone, I told my nephew that I must include his story in my own story because what he said is just too good to leave out!

It's Time to Lay it All Down

Some events that happen in life can take years before you can lay it all down. You talk about it, you share it because something significant happened to you. Experiencing situations such as being treated as less than valuable or feeling the sting of betrayal or suffering abuse as a young person are human experiences that not only took place a long time ago, they still take place today.

Some years ago, I met a young woman who told me her story. When she was very young, her mother forced her to marry the young man who impregnated her against her will. Unheard of to me in the society I grew up in, but it happens. While processing through the disruptive pain this created in her life and the pain of sometimes still suffering emotional mistreatment by her mother, she continues to love her mother dearly. Then there is the young man whose father emotionally traumatized him as a child by hurling insults and at times physically abusing him, yet refused to confess his wrongs. Threatening to do harm when this boy was very young if he shared his abusive story, what I see here are two adult people with a seared conscious inflicting pain on innocent children unable to defend themselves. I also see a mother more concerned with appearances than her daughter's emotional well-being. Both chose to disregard the embracing love a child needs. Parents do make mistakes, but abusers make choices to abuse and misuse. Childhood trauma can be hard to leave behind, but God's boundless love embracing a heart through expressions of love by others can heal the brokenhearted.

Everything we learn in life to benefit life amid the healing moments from past undeserved pain is often acquired over time. Oftentimes healing with no apologies. Simply saying "I'm sorry" is a sorry confession because as noted earlier, it begs the question, "Sorry for what?" It becomes hard to digest too when someone points a finger at you while blind to seeing the three fingers pointing back at them. They forgot about the pain they inflicted on your life, but then over time when you look back, as you brush the cobwebs away you remember things you experienced at their hands though remaining silent about it. What I began to see is that my love for them overshadowed their unprincipled behaviors. When you love deeply, you wash past hurts away that should have been dealt with because the residue remains. I find that people who love deeply, people who love innocently can bury someone else's wrong at the same time they are being frowned upon by that same person. Letting go is healing in the absence of an apology. Know that you are more than your pain and you are here because of God's love and His purpose for your life. Your life is precious in His sight.

Dancing in the rain is something I have learned to do because of the intimacy I feel about God's expressed love towards me. I danced in the rain in stormy seasons even before fully realizing the depth of His forgiveness. I realize now different events that take place in life can sometimes delay our learning in certain areas. For instance learning to forgive as Jesus forgave while processing through the pain of betrayal, abuse, loss, being cast aside or left behind and other such experiences can take time to process before fully letting go. I remember the day God changed the way I felt about those who I finally realized had less than the best intentions towards me. It can be a devasting blow to learn that some who are closest to you are the ones you really can't trust and are responsible for some of your greatest pain. But I am thankful for the day long ago when God brought me to the place where I prayed, "Lord forgive them for they know not what they do. Tap them a little but don't hurt them too much." Recognizing that God alone deals with injustices, I saw that God had changed the way I felt about those trapped in a cycle of hurling insults and betraying trust. The way I see it, when you genuinely love someone you care about how they feel and you also feel a responsibility to defend their value and character in the face of others who don't mind speaking illy of them. In other words, you don't sing with the choir. And you don't remain silent either because silence is a voice too. In these situations, silence is complicity. As Ida B. Wells articulated, "The way to right wrongs is to shine the light of truth on them."

Sin is an ugly thing. And words and actions unfiltered by the Holy Spirit brings separation when you begin to hold people accountable even if you temper your speech. I think sometimes about the truth of God's Word when it declares the things we do to one another are done to the Father which is a truth often placed on the shelf when a person doesn't want to be held accountable. But when you dust off this truth, repentance becomes necessary because when we join ourselves with God we become one with Him.[24] The thing about repentance is it includes confession whether confessing a matter is comfortable or not. In the Book of James, we are told to confess our sins one to another and to pray for one another that we may

---

24. I Corinthians 6:17.

be healed.²⁵ The way I see it, if you don't want a certain thing done to you, then don't do it to someone else. And if we have committed hurtful actions injuring someone's life, we apologize for that specific behavior. In the absence of an apology, we forgive anyway and when forgiving someone, it is not about excusing wrongful behavior. It comes down to obedience to God while it also protects our inner peace from carting emotional baggage. An eroding area in life that occurs quite often is conflict.

While putting the pieces of this story together, I just so happened to receive an email from In Touch Ministries titled "Confronting Conflict."²⁶ I saw the wisdom clothed inside insightful comments such as, "Painful disagreements are a part of living in this world—how we respond matters." This email ended with other penetrating truths when stating, "In the world, conflict is inevitable. When something we've done is the source of turmoil, we should apologize. If others are at fault, we should forgive. As Christ's ambassadors, the way we respond really matters." When apologizing to someone for our behavior, it is not simply a matter of saying, "I'm sorry" because as already mentioned, these two words beg the question—Sorry for what? When we are personally acquainted with God, a transformation has taken place. We are no longer the same. We care about the impact of our words spoken to others. And we care about our behavior. As also mentioned before, some things we learn take place over time.

Another area which is prevalent today and worth mentioning is a desire to fit in. Hopefully, we arrive at the place earlier than later in recognizing we don't fit in because we were born to stand apart and not to blend in. Living with a desire to fit in results in accepting behaviors that should have been confronted and corrected a long time ago. But then we find most folks don't want to be corrected. They don't like being called out on their behavior and will probably turn things around on you by saying you are being judgmental. I don't think they realize that God makes it very clear in His Word that we are to make righteous judgements so making judgements righteously is not being hypocritical. It is about correcting someone's behavior. When you realize things that displease the Holy Spirit displease the Father, it should also displease us too. Calling out a wrong is not done to make someone feel wounded when the heart is guided by right intentions. It is not done to condemn. It is not done to rub a person's nose

---

25. James 5:16.

26. Daily Devotion (online). Inspired by The Teachings of Charles F. Stanley. "Confronting Conflict." September 14, 2024.

in something committed in the past either. Because if what we voice to someone is carried out for these reasons, it doesn't reflect the heart of God. The motive is all wrong from the start. I have learned from an over 40 year close relationship, people definitely preach who they really are and we need to pay attention. Sometimes it may take a while to see it, but it is worth the journey of getting there, and I thank God for spiritual growth.

Something else I have come to understand is when you have been wronged, it is important to note in forgiving others it releases the one offended from emotional baggage. How good it is that God opens eyes to see that you don't have to be perfect to be perfect in how we show love towards one another. How good it is to understand when you are regarded as being different you may as well expect rejection. When you know your true value and you realize your self-worth, you stand up for what is right even when facing those you care deeply for. There can be righteous indignation about a matter that may help others see the truth.

When it comes to relationships, forgiving and loving someone doesn't require you to remain a part of the same circle when there is unrepentant behaviors. When the love you are receiving doesn't include accountability for disrespect, you will find yourself accepting unhealthy behaviors and the need to learn the lesson of letting go and placing someone in God's hands which can be a costly lesson when we don't let go. There are times when we make mistakes and God sees this too. He judges the intent of the heart. What is most important is what God sees and says about you. In agape love, you are not only useful as a friend, but valued as a person. Experiencing less than genuine love, I can only imagine how God must feel.

As mentioned earlier, when Jesus Christ walked the earth, oftentimes He walked alone with the Father. And He was rejected by those closest to Him. Though rejected by the masses, but accepted by the few, our Savior did not deviate from Who He was and is. Some people need to remain in your past.

This story you are reading is another story I thought I had finished, but God was not done yet. Weeks after I wrote it, I listened for a second time to Pastor Stephen Darby's online sermon *It's in The Family*. This time, I picked up on other insight as he explained forgiveness that brings out a bit more detail in my story. As Pastor Darby expressed, "Forgiveness takes courage. You have to release folk. You got to have courage to release. You got to let people go. It's a scary thing to look at what somebody has done to you and then say I forgive you. You don't wait for someone to come and

An Uphill Climb

tell you they're sorry. It may never happen."[27] And I add, forgiveness doesn't always result in reconciliation.

Several days later, I just so happened to read an InTouch Ministries Daily Devotion which also discussed forgiveness. Quoting from this online resource, it maintains, "Forgiveness is an act of the will more than an act of the heart. We don't often feel like showing mercy to someone who's wronged us—but that's exactly what we're called to do (Matt. 5:38–40)."[28]

Our Lord and Savior Jesus Christ hung on the cross and forgave it all for all mankind. For human beings this process can be challenging, but it's time to lay it all down. It is freeing to forgive, and if you are not free, it's time to free yourself. It is time to recognize that God sees who you are and He wants you know you are accepted and chosen the way He molded you to be. This doesn't mean we don't need to confess our sins one to another, but what it does mean for those who keep trying to fit in, you don't need to keep trying when the truth of the matter is the fabric you are made from is different than the character of those in that circle where you don't fit. For any disconcerting matters that may have happened in your life, it's time to free yourself of a burden belonging to the offender, not the offended. God is the ultimate Judge. Wouldn't want it any other way. How good it is to learn something more about knowing the heart of God.

It is Apostle Paul who proclaimed in the Book of Romans our heavenly Father's kindness and mercy leads one to repentance.[29] Paul's spoken words follow with a warning that a stubborn heart will experience judgment which leads us to call out unrighteous behaviors. Prayer is so needed today to open the eyes of spiritual blindness. Along our journey, we find that learning about the Bible and learning more about God and our need to grow to look more like our Savior is helped through discipleship where we grow in understanding in how to apply the words of our Savior when He proclaimed, "My food is to do the will of Him who sent Me, and to accomplish His work."[30]

---

27. Steven Darby Ministries (online sermon). *It's In The Family (Message)*. April 22, 2013.

28. Daily Devotion (online). Inspired by The Teachings of Charles F. Stanley. "Victory Over Unforgiveness." November 20, 2024.

29. Romans 2:4.

30. John 4:34. (NASB95).

Something About Knowing God

God is our bridge over troubled water. He is our saving grace, our shelter from the storm, our confidant, our way maker, our Prince of Peace. Lord, I thank You for Your help to lay it all down.

> Hebrews 10:24. And let us consider one another in order to stir up love and good works. (NJKV)

Chapter 3

Timely Reflections

The Place Where We Are

WHERE DO YOU SEE yourself today? Is the place you see yourself a tough spot in life? Or is it a place where you have healed from old wounds, or do you see yourself in the process of healing? Maybe you are in a place of waiting for doors to open to move you beyond where you are now. If this is where you happen to be, has God spoken to your heart about something you need to trust Him for? Wherever you are on your journey, all of us are in God's hands though many of us are awaiting His timing to change the direction of our circumstances. I have discovered when facing less than ideal circumstances, God sets up moments in time when we need to cry out to Him. But He also sends us to places where somebody needs His light to shine to bring hope to a downtrodden spirit or to open the eyes of the spiritual blind and He will even use us in our broken state to do it. Whatever circumstance we happen to encounter while carrying out a God-assignment or while simply going about daily life it beckons us to trust God for an unforeseen outcome. Recall for a moment when Jesus told Peter and the disciples who were with him to get into the boat to go ahead of Him to the other side while He sent the multitude away. What happened? Jesus did not come to save them until the fourth watch[1] which meant He did not come the first, the second or the third watch. Jesus purposely waited until the fourth watch. For Peter and the disciples walking with him this meant

---

1. Matthew Chapter 14, Verse 22.

Something About Knowing God

they had to struggle before Christ arrived on the scene to rescue them from a situation He had already planned. This reminds me of some words of wisdom I once heard—faith not tested cannot be trusted.

No matter the length of time one has walked with God, every faith journey is filled with ebbing tides and rising currents and doubts and despair in the midst of hope and joy. So it is worth recognizing if we've changed much in our level of faith and trust in God since first coming to know Him. Some may not have changed at all, but I believe it is worth realizing if we have grown to be wholly dependent upon God in trying seasons, or do we continue to lean on our own understanding. It is worth recognizing whether we run to others for help before we run to God. It is worth identifying if we still find ourselves caught up in worry though God has never failed us. Some of us, I believe, can raise our hands here. I have often found before God's perfect plan comes to light, our situation will often appear in total disarray so patience plays a crucial role in our journey as we wait for God to overturn draining circumstances . God is moving while we wait. He is healing us, transforming us. Preparing us to receive His blessings. When we are able to wholeheartedly trust that God's perfect timing will bring order out of chaos we can hold on to His promise to deliver. So where do you find yourself today?

In my journey with God there has been times He has led me to places I surely would not have chosen for myself. At least not initially. But God brought insight to sightless eyes to know that He can be trusted in places quite foreign to me. Places that do not mirror anything at all like anything I have experienced in my past. While struggling with something foreign and quite unfamiliar, our hearts can fill with deep concern and even alarm. This sounds exactly like many stories we've read about in the Bible where God purposely led His people into uncharted territory only for them to realize it was always His perfect plan. The beauty of it all back then and for us today is lives were and are changed when confronting the unfamiliar. Just think about the times the Lord's disciples walked into a foreign territory for the first time and people were set free. Chains fell off and bonds were broken freeing people from years of captivity. Though God brings His people safely to the other side, it is not without facing opposing circumstances while we follow in the footsteps of His only begotten Son.

This brings to mind the time when God had me work inside an all-male prison though I pleaded with Him not to send me there, but He did anyway. I could see no good reason why God would send me to a place where He knew I would be afraid. And I struggled to understand why He would send me to a place where I would be confined behind walls where terrible fights would sometimes break out and where I would often find myself walking the prison yard alone without a single guard in sight. It took me a while, but the fear left as I saw lives change for the better. Although I did meet with a few obstacles, mostly the obstacles arose because of the prison guards and not because of the prisoners. All the while, I saw God's power to protect and to keep me safe while serving as His instrument of change for many locked behind a tall barbed-wire fence. I believe God's intent in sending me to work there was partly because He saw the hearts of those needing to witness care through an earthen vessel molded to make a difference despite the crime. And also because I needed to trust God in unfamiliar territory and to learn the value in simply voicing, "Why not me? Lord thank You for using me," a few words not often spoken when enduring the unfamiliar.

Had it not been for the hard places of opposition and struggles in life, I would not have come to better understand something more about knowing God personally, and I would not have known how to walk with Him during silent moments or in silent seasons of time. I would not have gained insight from life's storms which seemed so disfavorable when all the while God is working out everything for our good. Had it not been for God's incredible deliverances at times when I thought all hope was gone and experiences that filled me with testimonies giving praise to His name, I would not have life stories to write about nor would I know how to bring words of hope to the brokenhearted nor how to come alongside experiences we all have in common. From words of my inspired declaration expressed in my previous book, I say to you too—"If I made it through, so can you." Working inside the walls of a male prison turned out to be one of the best jobs I ever had.

In times of feeling desperation or despair while following or striving to follow after God's own heart, trust that His assignment has brought you to the very place where you are now. Even as we struggle with our own circumstance, God takes note of those around us who need His help and He knows just who to send. Places that appear larger than life I've found are the very places God intends to win the battle just as He did for Jehoshaphat.

On March 13, 1988, at 4:20 a.m., I couldn't sleep so I began to talk to God about facing an enemy bigger than me. I confessed to God I didn't want to confront this enemy if He didn't go with Me. I admitted I didn't know what to do, and I also confessed to God, "My eyes are on You." I believe God peered inside my heart because He led me to read a familiar Scripture where I perceived my current situation was being addressed. Just as the story in Second Chronicles reveals, God's people did not have to engage in battle,[2] and by the grace of God nor did I because God delivered me out of the hands of the enemy before anything happened.

More recently, God allowed me to face yet another larger than life situation when a close friend confided battling an unhealthy addiction. God caused me to remember His delivering power as He once again led me to read the same story in Second Chronicles He led me to read in 1988 when I was facing my own personal dilemma. While praying and fasting for my friend, not only did God again lead me to read the same story in Second Chronicles, but He also had me to reflect on something I wrote on June 1st, 1991. This happened to be the day God nudged my heart to read Isaiah Chapter 58, Verses 6 through 8 which speaks to fasting and praying. It was while reading these verses of Scripture in the Book of Isaiah, for the first time God opened my eyes to see the importance of fasting and praying when a situation is urgent. So while praying for my friend's problem as I had done on previous occasions, this time for three days I fasted and prayed while reflecting on the time almost 35 years ago in 1991 when God spoke to me when He delivered me out of my own predicament through fasting and praying. Amazingly, while recently fasting and praying for my friend, on the second day I witnessed God's redeeming power at work. And on the third day, God unexpectedly reminded me of Queen Esther's call to fast and pray for three days found in the Book of Esther in the Old Testament. I understood that God was reassuring my heart that He was answering my prayer for my friend. Surely, God knows how to connect the dots in the Bible to let us know He is here with us. As noted before, I believe the stories in the Bible reveal life messages for situations we face today. Some things come out only by fasting and praying.

God is still the same yesterday, today, and forevermore. All that we are and all that we have been given—our giftings and our talents—God gives to us to use for His glory to serve the wellbeing of those around us. We learn in life along with triumphs comes suffering and suffering should give us the heart to hear others' pain just as God hears ours.

While we are still here, our story is not done yet. God builds something greater in us as we yield ourselves to Him. Even if faltering along the way, God saw you before you fell and His unlimited compassion and

---

2. Second Chronicles, Chapter 20, Verse 17.

grace can restore and transform whatever needs fixing. He made you and He knows how to take care of your past and your future and the place where you are now. If you're waiting and anticipating for God to show up and the path seems to be blocked, then it's not the right time yet. Though often hard to wait God's timing, I had to learn God for myself to know His best is yet to come. God sometimes reserves the best for last as told in another story in this book. Lord, I thank you for Your best to come in this season of life for Your chosen vessels. At the time when You do come through, the outcome is always better than we expected.

> Isaiah 43:19. See, I am doing a *new thing*! Now it springs up; do you not perceive it? I am making a way in the wilderness and streams in the wasteland. (NIV; emphasis mine)
>
> Romans 8:28. And we know that all things work together for good to those who love God, to those who are the called according to *His* purpose. (NKJV)

God is Intentional

From the dust of the ground God formed man in His own image. Intentional. Concerning His divine purpose for creating each life, intentional. Intentional when it comes to all that concerns you and me as His servant David declared.[3] God is intentional when it comes to the path He leads us to walk upon. Intentional when He opens the eyes of our understanding to recognize something unknown to us before about who He is. About His name, His glory, His love, His presence, His character, and His story as revealed through you and me. God is intentional when He touches a heart to rise in renewed hope while surrounded by troubling waters. Intentional when His favor blooms in our lives to touch the lives of others. There is not one season under the sun where God does not intend to reveal His unseen but glorious presence as He orchestrates earthly matters that tell of His limitless power. While we live out His divine plan here on earth, God shows us that we don't have to be perfect to be perfectly used by Him. He opens the eyes of our understanding to recognize that we can still finish strong while He continues to mold us to look more like His Son.

Let's consider again the life of Peter. Although Peter denied knowing our Savior three times, God still used him mightily to proclaim the message of His only begotten Son, Jesus Christ. So don't look at yourself as worse than your worse failure. If your life looks anything like Peter's rugged beginning or maybe like Apostle Paul who had a thorn in his flesh, as it happened with Apostle Paul, if God doesn't remove the thorn, He gives grace sufficient to live with something we wanted gone yesterday. He is still the same God who reveals His amazing grace and boundless love all clothed within a heart of compassion intent on blessing His people.

This reminds me of a time when I had no previous insight that a negatively charged situation would soon unfold right before my eyes as I walked quietly down the street. It happened to me while in my early thirties when I was employed by a major bank and was scheduled to attend training at one of the bank's San Francisco locations. Not being acquainted with the area, I was not at all prepared for what would soon unfold. However, I came to understand that God had already prepared to shield me from an unexpected situation headed my way. While walking alone towards the bank's training center, I suddenly sensed someone was following me so I glanced behind me and saw a young man walking not too far in the distance. To

---

3. Psalm 138:8.

know for sure if he was following me, I crossed the street and immediately, he crossed the street too. Feeling a bit unnerved and not knowing what to do, I began to walk faster and when I glanced behind me again, his pace had also quickened. Only God could have set up the moment I am about to share with you. Not far ahead of me, there happened to be an older businessman waiting at the corner for the traffic light to change, and he just so happened to be headed in my same direction. Walking briskly up to him, I stopped and began a conversation with him as though I'd known him before. While we talked and waited for the light to change, the young man following me stopped about five feet behind us, and he waited too. When the light changed, I continued talking with this businessman as we crossed the intersection, and when I glanced behind me a third time, the young man who had been following me was now walking in the opposite direction. He must have thought I knew this businessman, but I didn't. After explaining to this man the situation I had just encountered, he offered to walk me to the bank's training center and he saw me safely inside. In my early thirties, I had just experienced something about God I had not known before—He saves us when we don't even know we need saving. God is intentional when it comes to His chosen people. Only God could have set up this perfect moment for me to meet this businessman.

Throughout the Bible, we see God leading His people through unchartered territory. From events lived out in the Bible, we gain insight and wisdom to face challenges today as we connect with meaningful reflections to call to mind when we encounter unfamiliar situations we've not met with before. One lesson we can learn from those who lived years ago during biblical times is not to balk at or to give reason to excuse ourselves when God calls us to do something bigger than we think we are capable of handling. Thoughts come to mind of Moses, and Jonah, and Barak the son of Abinoam because all three of these men did this very thing I just mentioned not to do, just as I have often found myself doing. I find this same spirit alive today.

It is good to remember that God remains intentional when He takes us into unfamiliar territory. I must admit, had I known that young man was going to follow me, I would not have gone to the bank's training center. And neither would I have worked inside an all-male prison years later. But I know enough now to realize that God protects and provides when He calls us to walk uncharted paths. There is work for us to do and knowledge God intends to reveal to us about who He is as He makes us aware of personal behaviors and attitudes that need to change. God is also intentional when He saves the best for last too. Not too long ago, He had me learn a spiritual lesson behind an inconsequential earthly matter.

Recently, I attended a social function where every attendee received a ticket with a number that would later be called upon to receive a free gift. Time was allotted for us to look over the items so we could decide beforehand which gift to choose when our number was called. Having made my decision along with another woman who sat at my table, we both hoped for our number to be called in time to receive our chosen gift. Wouldn't you know that her number was called early enough for her to receive her chosen gift, but as for me, my number was one of the last ones called. Every woman sitting at my table had already had their number called and all of them received their desired gift. When the number belonging to the woman sitting to my left was announced, she chose the gray purse with the sophisticated handle that had been my gift of choice. Puzzled, I thought to myself, *this is not like God for me*. While still waiting for my number to be called, the woman sitting to my right nudged me and asked, "Isn't that the purse you wanted?" "Yes, but it's okay," I replied. In my mind I had already formed the thought, *Somebody else maybe for the first time needs to go first or second or even third*. Not knowing what God had planned for me, the only other item I remembered seeing was a brown and tan vase. But as I said before, God is intentional! As I walked up towards the front to select my free gift, laughingly I announced to the smiling audience, "God has saved the best for last for me!" while not realizing this is exactly what God had done for me. We all laughed behind what I had cheerily announced. On the table of gifts there just happened to be another gray purse that I had not noticed before. It was much larger in size than the one I had initially chosen. This larger gray purse turned out to be exactly the purse I needed! I had to smile to myself when I realized that the straps of this larger purse could be placed easily over my shoulder instead of having to carry a smaller purse in my hand. I beamed at the fact that all of my needed items could fit snuggly inside this larger purse which I would have been unable to do with the smaller gray one. And to top it all off, this larger gray purse is also very appealing to the eye. All the while God knew the exact purse that would work best for me. He intentionally allowed someone else to go before me to choose the purse I thought I needed which would have been a purse much too small for my personal use. No longer do I need to keep using my two keepsake cloth purses that I plan to pass on to my granddaughters.

God used this simple earthly matter to send me a spiritual message—sometimes He saves the best for last. So while you wait for God's promises to unfold, just as it was credited to saving the best wine for last at a wedding in Cana of Galilee[4] which happens to be a place where Jesus manifested His glory,[5] the same thing happens for us too. God is intentional when He saves the best for last when choosing the options that will work best for your life and mine. Oh how we need to trust the God of the Bible. As I write these words, I am in such a place right now. How about you?

> I Peter 3:15. but sanctify Christ as Lord in your hearts, always being ready to make a defense to everyone who asks you to give an account for the hope that is in you, yet with gentleness and reverence; (NASB95)

---

4. John 2:10.
5. John 2:11.

Learning To be Happy in Your Storm

A few stories back, I spoke about dancing in the rain, but this particular story brings a somewhat different flavor to understanding what it means to survive in hard times. Joining together the word "happy" and the word "storm" may sound a bit opposing but actually, the word "happy" as it appears in the Bible can be translated blessed. The word happy can also be defined as joy and fulfillment. So in keeping with this mindset, we can be happy, cheerful, content and realize that we are blessed in stormy weather because we still have life so we can choose to disallow the storm to determine our level of inner peace.

Not all stormy weather is the same either. Sometimes we encounter a twister-like storm that swiftly hits and quickly vanishes from sight though it still can bring immeasurable loss. In these storms we seek to find comfort in God as our Healer. At other times there is a succession of storms that seem to tear at the very fiber of life causing shed tears and mounting questions and earnest cries to God to end the storms that just seem to keep coming. Then there are times when God allows storms to clean out old things no longer needed or to remove things that should never have occupied space in our lives in the first place. But no matter the kind of storm encountered, storms don't tell the whole story. Although they can bring immeasurable loss, storms can't determine the final outcome. While we still live and breathe, we can acknowledge that we are blessed because we are still here to carry out whatever plans God has predestined for our lives. In my journey with God, I've often experienced God turning the worst of circumstances around to reveal His presence and to benefit my future just as I mentioned in the previous story. Something else I've discovered in the midst of challenging moments is God always makes room for a time of rest, for a time of refreshment that allows us to refocus our thoughts while we recall His words of hope that strengthen our faith and as we recall the many places He's delivered us from. Apostle Paul in the Book of Philippians reminds us to remember uplifting words of affirmation when he proclaims, "Finally, brethren, whatever is true, whatever is honorable, whatever is right, whatever is pure, whatever is lovely, whatever is of good repute, if there is any excellence and if anything worthy of praise, let your mind dwell on these things."[6] Sometimes when weathering a railing storm, we need to change our focus.

---

6. Philippians 4:8. (NASB95).

One day many years ago, my oldest son called me at work and said, "Mom, there are only three types of people: Those coming out of a storm, those in a storm, and those on their way to a storm. Only these three types of people. So one of them is you and one of them is the person sitting next to you and one of them is me too! Storms are a part of life whether we want them to be or not. I am afraid to say they are here to stay until we leave this place. Until we leave this life!" In quoting my son's words, you probably realize the same thing I do about storms—storms don't get any easier. And they don't go away. And the older we get, storms seem to pick up speed, size and momentum. Upon realizing that trials are a natural part of life, we may as well learn how to endure them in a way that benefit us mentally, emotionally, and spiritually.

We can truly miss what God intends for us to learn when things appear in total disarray if not paying attention. So we must strive not to allow the enemy to leave our lives in an emotional shamble. Ultimately, the situations we encounter not only develop us spiritually and emotionally, but as a result of learning while enduring storms, we become equipped to help others transition through their stormy life season. We don't generally think this way when hit with something unforeseen and unwelcomed because the first thought that readily comes to mind is, "Stop the storm, Lord. It's been enough." But if God ended every storm in life when we desire it to end, there would be a lot of us walking around spiritually undeveloped and ill equipped to help others to trust God who does complete work. Kicking and screaming as we do sometimes, God finishes what He starts.

While we walk through life, we learn that storms provide opportunities to deepen our trust and faith in God and to experience God in ways that develop an understanding that would not have been possible without encountering storms. I've learned that storms can serve as a catalyst to bring us closer to our destiny. I wish I'd known this a long time ago because it would have helped me to better accept the difficult places God would allow entry into my life. They proved to be crucial for my personal and spiritual development to write life stories that help others be encouraged and filled with hope. Stories that praise His great name. Had I known beforehand, I would have rested a bit better when facing the unfamiliar.

Accepting that God is intentional about everything He does from start to finish helps us to let go and to be led by His Holy Spirit regardless of the storm we face. Walking in renewed hope lessens anxiousness and helps us to find contentment in the space we happen to be when we realize there are many people who don't have the safety and resources we have at our disposal just as I witnessed the other day. Looking out over world events, the need to pray for others continues even when our own life is shaken just as it was for David and for others who came before our time.

I want to mention the part of David's life again when he ran from King Saul. Talk about a storm! The trials that David encountered were different storms that extended for years and not just days. It was tough on David, but because he experienced a multitude of stormy seasons, we have his beautiful psalms that inspire us today. Were his storms easy? No. But did they serve a purpose? Yes. David was molded into a courageous warrior and a man after God's own heart, the man God knew he would become.

Now take Joseph who was sold into slavery by his own brothers. Talk about betrayal! And Joseph's storms were also experienced over a number of years. Though betrayed, sent to prison and lied upon, God had purpose in mind for Joseph while Joseph suffered. After his storms ended, Joseph was promoted to second in command next to the Pharaoh who ruled in his day. God used Joseph in a mighty way to save the lives of countless people enduring a famine that stretched across the land. Even to save his own family who betrayed him. Throughout the Bible we see the same pattern—those battling with heartache and doubt and an array of troubles only to be led later to serve a greater purpose. God is never wrong, sometimes misunderstood, but He is never wrong.

Another thing about storms is storms test us. They prove our faith. Storms move things out of our lives and move other things into our lives as mentioned earlier. Storms come in different sizes for different lengths of time. But there are a few things about a storm that remain the same: You have to go through a storm—you can't go around it—you can't go over it, and you can't wish it away. You must go through it. A second thing is—we are not coming out of a storm until we have completed the reason for being *in* the storm. The third thing is storms are hurtful experiences.

In my dictionary, the word *storm* is explained using these words: "A natural storm is an atmospheric disturbance manifested in strong winds accompanied by some other natural elements. And the winds of a storm can range from 64 to 72 miles per hour. A storm can also be described as a shower of heavy objects such as bullets and missiles."[7] My dictionary also mentioned a storm can be a violent disturbance or upheaval or a

---

7. The American Heritage Dictionary. Second College Edition. 1982. Houghton Mifflin Company.

violent, sudden attack on a fortified place. So the very nature of a natural storm is to meant to be chaotic, unrestrained, unrelenting, and unmanageable which seemingly parallels our own life experiences when weathering a rough patch. We face strong winds of adversity, some heavy showers of opposition and sometimes even violent attacks upon our credibility, our testimony, and even our faith. Pain can cause us to withdraw, to curl up and to isolate ourselves and this can be one of the worst things to do if done over a prolonged period of time because we can cut off opportunities to be encouraged and comforted by others who God intends to use to reach out to us. But then there are times when we are to be alone to ourselves with only God at our side. In times like these, when He opens a door, I find He knows just who to send.

Like David, encouraging ourselves in the Lord our God is vital. And putting on the garment of praise for a spirit of heaviness changes our focus. We can have inner peace amid life's storms when we remind ourselves that God is the same yesterday, today and forevermore and when we remind ourselves that God has intentionally declared this statement and posed this question: "Behold, I am the Lord, the God of all flesh; is anything too difficult for Me?"[8] And He answers His own question in the amazing displays of His intervening power to bring deliverance to change situations during biblical times and in times we face today.

God is the same God today He was to Daniel in the lion's den, to Shadrach, Meshack and Abendego in the fiery furnace and to Paul and Silas and other apostles when held captive inside a prison cell. He has not lost His power to deliver. He sees and plans where we're headed before we get there, and He also sees man's intended interruptions. Though in countless situations we see the free will of man on display, we also recognize that God knows when and how to deliver His people. When God allows troubling waters to surface and erode the land, He still has a plan. So the next time you find yourself struggling with why God hasn't delivered you out of a troubling dilemma, remember these words spoken in Habakkuk 2:3 where the man of God declares, "Though it tarries, wait for it, for it will surely come." God has not changed. We can't push Him ahead of what's on His calendar. And since our happiness is not found because *of* the storm, but because of knowing who God is *in* the storm, sometimes I think instead of concentrating on the deliverance we so desperately seek, maybe we need to concentrate on what God is trying to show us. Maybe we need to focus

---

8. Jeremiah 32:27 (NASB95).

more on God and to thank Him for what He's already done. It serves us better to focus on the vertical anyway rather than the horizontal because there are just too many memories of God being for us not to find something to be joyous and thankful about in our present circumstance. Fittingly quoting from one of Dr. David Jeremiah's Turning Points devotionals I had tucked away many years ago, Dr. David Jeremiah asserted, "What we are until we suffer is merely reputation; what we are while we suffer is character. Reputation is what men think you are; character is what God knows you are."

Lastly, reflecting on Paul's words to be content in every situation, if you research the word *content* it means satisfaction and satisfaction is all wrapped up in happiness. The word "joy" itself means happiness or great pleasure. In John, Chapter Ten, Verse 10, Jesus declares that He desires for us to enjoy life and have life in abundance. Our Savior went on to express in Chapter Fifteen, Verse 11 that He wants His joy and delight to be in us so that our joy and gladness will be of a full measure. Jesus also emphasized that we are to have His gladness within us filling our hearts.

In the Amplified Bible, the word "happy" applies to whoever leans on, trusts in, and is confident in the Lord. "Happy blessed and fortunate is he," are words written in the Amplified Bible which to me sounds relational, not circumstantial. So the secret to being happy is depending upon God to meet our daily needs which erases anxiousness of thought. Happiness is not to be based solely upon a new job or a new home or some other aspiration attained. It has to resonate from something deep within which I believe correctly corresponds to the words of Proverbs 15, Verse 13 where it is proclaimed, "A joyful heart makes a cheerful face but when the heart is sad, the spirit is broken."[9] As also reaffirmed by these words, "A joyful heart is good medicine, but a broken spirit dries up the bones."[10] Both Scriptures indicate that joy and happiness meet up with each other. The question for us is where do we find ourselves emotionally and spiritually in the circumstances we wanted gone yesterday?

> Habakkuk 3:19. The Lord God is my strength, and He has made my feet like hinds' feet, and makes me walk on my high places. (NASB95)

---

9. New American Standard Bible (1995).
10. Proverbs 17:22. (NASB95).

Timely Reflections
Power in the Name

The name of the Lord is a strong tower; the righteous run to Him and are safe.[11] To live above experiencing trying times of worry and doubt, we should strive to allow these profound words of truth to settle deep within our soul. Sometimes we run to others first when experiencing stressful situations, and I don't think we realize in that moment where our help really comes from. At any given time, no matter whose hand God uses to help us, it is still His love and power motivating the person who helps us to bring us through times of despair. Being mindful of where our power truly comes from keeps us pointing to God rather than to ourselves in all things we set out to accomplish.

I marvel at God when I think of the millions of people in the world and His ability to watch over every single person at all times and to speak to each individual heart. Now that's power! "Who is this great God we serve?" I ask myself. He is God who created the heavens and the earth. He is God who parted the waters of the Red Sea and caused the waters of the Jordan River to stand up in a heap allowing His people to cross over on dry land. He is God who performs wonders in the wilderness which is still experienced in some form today. He is God who sits high but sees down below. The God we can call on and rely on. The God who saves you and me. The God mankind is called to serve.

When God is in our midst, so is deliverance. When He is the anchor of our hope so is His peace there with us that defies human logic. I often think of times we strive to get things to work out our way when all the time we should be trusting God to work out things His way. There is power in His name. There is deliverance in His name. There is salvation in His name. Though hardships befall us, and although we may not understand many of the attributes of God's divine nature and His timing to set things in motion, He remains seated on His throne reigning in absolute power. God remains able and willing to handle all situations concerning you and me. He knows when and how to deal with those in power too.

In life, one encounter we often find is conflict. It's all over the world. Today more than any other time in history, I've seen and probably you've witnessed, we need the power of God to break through nationally and in family conflicts. Thank God for His only begotten Son our Lord and Savior

---

11. Proverbs 18:10. (NKJV).

Something About Knowing God

Jesus Christ who brought us to the throne room of grace where our help comes from. Oh, how we need Him today in such turbulent times.

We can learn many invaluable lessons from the wandering years of God's chosen people. One detail that sticks out in my mind that is expounded upon in Psalm 78 is when Scripture reveals God's chosen people forgetting about His past deeds and miracles as they murmured and complained in His presence.[12] It still sounds like us today. Their story sends a clear message not to follow in their same pattern of behavior of forgetting the power of God's name and His past deliverances, but rather call to mind that God is omnipresent, omnipotent, and omniscient. He is God Almighty who changes the battle in our favor and who steps over the voice of man when man says, "No." We should call to mind the God who knows how to bend unyielding knees. The God who sets up kings and takes kings down. The God who asks the question, "Is anything too difficult for Me?" The only true and living God who fills our hearts with renewed hope and Who serves as our moral compass. El Shaddai who looks our way and conditions change. Yahweh Nissi, the God who fights for His people. Adonai, His name to remind us of His authority. Elohim, His name indicating His sovereignty. Yeshua, His name that signifies to rescue or deliver. Names which are included among all the names that speak of God's character, His divine nature and His eternal and mighty power. The enemy of our soul knows well the boundless authority of God's name. It is good for us to remember this the next time the enemy knocks on our door. Even in moments of peace we should stand prepared, always relying on the power of His great name in the place where we are.

> I Corinthians 2:5. that your faith should not rest on the wisdom of men, but on the power of God. (NASB95)

---

12. Psalm 78:11. (NASB95).

Timely Reflections

No Greater Love

No greater love do we have than the love we receive from our heavenly Father. Stop for a moment and ponder the years of your life. Consider all the places you've been where God brought you through when you thought you weren't going to make it. Consider the hardships you've encountered that are sprinkled with the sweet scent of victory because of His great name. Reflect on Who brought you through both the good and the dark times. Look about God's creation and see His love for all mankind. Everything needed to bring solace to the heart lies in full display before our eyes in His awesome creation where I found and wrote about beauty in moments that many may overlook.[13] From all that God created, only man did God make in His own image. What great love God has bestowed upon mankind. What great love He displays through His power to deliver, to transform, and to make whole again. What great love does God reveal through His invisible presence. No greater love can we experience.

For God so loved the world He gave His only begotten Son. So everything we do for others should express the hand of God reaching out to them. His great love should be exercised not only in the way we treat one another, but in exercising our gifts and talents. Recently, I heard a local pastor comment, "Love is not in the manifestation of the gifts and talents so graciously bestowed upon us. But instead, whatever we do in using our gifts and talents must be motivated by love."[14] So it mustn't be that we use our gifts and talents to showcase what God has so graciously bestowed upon us. It mustn't be to receive acclamation from others either. Instead, everything we do with all that we've been graciously given by God should be used to glorify His name. To make His name known. A good question to ask ourselves is, "What motivates us to do what we do before God's people?"

When it comes to the love we show one another, have you ever been confused by someone's affection and mistakenly thought of it as love? We learn that true love which is agape love is living love. It is in our walk and in our talk which takes it beyond mere affection and mere emotion. Sure, you can feel love, but true love is an expression that *always* does. It's limitless. True love or agape love is not random in its actions, not infrequent, but it lives every day. Agape love is the thread that should run throughout one's lifestyle. This kind of love is consistent, not casual. It is genuine love

---

13. Taken from my book, *Your Creation Declares Your Glory!*
14. Pastor C. Sweeney. Online sermon. September 22, 2024. *Love, the Greatest of All.*

which loves at all times. Genuine love stems from thinking of others and their needs first, and not always first thinking about our own needs. Sure we exercise wisdom because genuine love is not acting without God's leading. And if you mess up, you fess up. You can be anointed and appointed but your love might not look like the Father's love because God's love is ever flowing and unending. God's love compels us to look in the mirror. So unless the reason we do what we do is motivated by genuine love, true to I Corinthians 13:1, we have become a clanging symbol or a noisy gong. Enough can't be said about genuine love because everything God does is motivated by agape love. The world will know we are true followers of Christ Jesus by the love we show one another. So as we consider our relationships, how do you think we are doing with this today? If you've ever experienced less than genuine love in what you thought was a close and perhaps family bond, imagine how God must feel.

Reflecting again on the pastor's sermon mentioned above, he also spoke on Galatians 5:22. He remarked that we should take notice the word fruit is *singular*. And also to notice what the fruit of the Holy Spirit looks like. It looks like God and it is a byproduct of knowing His Son Jesus Christ. As this pastor further expressed, "The fruit of the Spirit in us is love." Therefore love and the Holy Spirit are tied together as he rightly concluded. And we cannot have one without the other. So when it comes to love, Galatians 5:22 along with Galatians 5:23 is our checklist. It is our gauge to measure ourselves. It is most likely not the great message being preached by the church today, and sometimes it is missing in leadership circles inside the church where you might experience being excluded by smiling faces that lets you know you don't belong. Be thankful that you don't because God's love should be reflected in the outpouring of affection shown to our neighbors and our families in our homes and inside the church where the demonstration of love should not be exclusive but inclusive. God's love was never about titles, but it was and is about His glory poured out through vessels of clay using His gifts that are ever flowing through us. This reminds me of something I heard at a local church service when the guest speaker commented that the church needs to hear through the voice of others who are not well-known. I think she saw this was missing within this particular church because I saw it too. It was all about titles and degrees and prestige. Going back to considering the needs of others, we can learn from Scriptures such as Titus 3:14 where we are admonished, "Our people must learn to do good by meeting the urgent needs of others." (NLT)

Timely Reflections

Much can be learned from the Thirteenth Chapter of First Corinthians as well. In this chapter, the Bible declares that no matter the gifts we have, the greatest gift is love. And if we read further on, Chapter Fourteen instructs us to pursue love. But as mentioned in a previous story, loving someone does not mean to remain on the receiving end of harmful behaviors and unhealthy communication.

When we reflect on God's love as displayed by His servant David, and Gideon and Moses, and Noah, and Father Abraham, and Joshua, and Prophetess Deborah, along with a host of downtrodden and hurting people and among many of those we read about in the New Testament, we see God's hand of mercy extended above their own circumstance. Throughout the Bible we see God's love bigger than anything we can put into words or can be measured by any man-made instrument. When we look over our own lives and reflect on the lives of loved ones, and as we listen to others' testimonies and while reflecting on the places God has brought us through, it rings with this resounding truth—No greater love. God's love stretches wide and runs deep without measure. His love should be the motivator behind the actions we take and also before the words we speak. And when it doesn't, we should pause long enough to make things right. The love we show one another reveals whether we love the way God loves as declared in John 15:12. Love requires accountability.

Speaking about God's love, I see the Bible as a love letter to the church. God gave His only begotten Son as a sacrifice for you and me to live eternally in His presence. Only a loving Father would bring us this far from where we first began. So moved by seeing the word love repeatedly mentioned in the Bible, I researched it and found that love is mentioned 686 times in the NIV Bible, 504 times in the NKJV Bible, and 566 in the Amplified Bible Classic Edition. God has a lot to say about love. The way we love one another is huge and it speaks volumes about our relationship with God.

Inside the covers of this book, I hope you have seen God using another one of His ordinary clay vessels to speak about more than a few of His life changing messages. I hope you have witnessed God's compassion for man and His desire to answer prayer in many of my life stories you have read. Also, I hope you realize Your own stories are worth sharing.

> I John 4:9-10. In this the love of God was made manifest toward us, that God sent His only Son into the world, so that we might live through Him. (NKJV)

Something About Knowing God

I John 4:7. Beloved, let us love one another, for love is of God; and everyone who loves is born of God and knows God. (NKJV)

Timely Reflections

In memory of my loving mother Ruth Berry:

Mama

Mama. A face like an angel, a heart full of love.
God took you home and you're smiling now from heaven above.
Your legacy still reaches out to me.
Though years have passed, your sweet face I still see.

Mama. The love of my life. A sweet spirit surrounds you too.
Your gentle ways I hold onto in my constant remembrance of you.
Mama. A face like an angel, a heart full of love.
Something I remember you were always so full of.

Your journey was short lived on this green earth.
God saw your heart wanting to be with the children you birthed.
But He took you home relieving you of your pain and your struggles.
No more burdens now from heartbreaking troubles.

Your loving daughter, Vera

It's Just God's Way

Quoting from the Bible, "In the whirlwind and storm is His way."[15]

I remember the day I bent down to look for something inside a cabinet underneath a bathroom sink. My heart was so weighed down from experiencing one hardship after another. I couldn't figure out why God was allowing such heart wrenching moments to pummel my life that looked like defeat. Because my heart was so torn, I grew silent before the Lord. But God broke through the silence to reveal that He knew exactly what I was feeling because in that very moment, I heard Him say, "Vera you have been hearing from Me all along but you are afraid to trust Me because of the devastation and constant tearing that has occurred in your life." And He was right. Viewing life through a spiritual lens, later I came to realize that out of turbulent circumstances allowed by God's hand emerges the strength to endure and the fortitude to overcome whatever we are facing while living life on earth as we know it today.

This brings to mind God's servant Job. God answered Job out of a whirlwind. And a whirlwind is mentioned again when God took Elijah up to heaven. I think of other places in the Bible where a whirlwind is mentioned to indicate God's presence and His power, and sometimes His judgment. When it comes to a great number of things that God allows to take place in our lives, the outcome can benefit others in our written and spoken message as we call to mind God's presence and His power to overcome no matter the turbulent storms that brew. At times when we feel that God could have handled some things a bit differently to prevent us from going through what we went through, we can think of Job and a host of others. As mentioned earlier, everything God does or allows to happen in life is purposeful, even though many times it is hurtful. While we walk this earth, God shapes us for the destiny He has called us to live. And He also knows when it is time to bring us home to live eternally with Him.

Thinking about Father Abraham's journey on this earth, it stretched for many years. His journey leading to father a son was a long one, but his son Issac was born at just the right time. Abraham was 75 years of age when God told him he would have a son, then ten years passed by and no son was born to him and his wife Sarah. After twenty-five years Isaac was born and Scripture reveals that Isaac held the blessing of God. In the whirlwind and the storm is God's way as His purpose is fulfilled. Although Abraham's and

---

15. Nahum 1:3b. (NASB95).

Sarah's waiting time might differ from our own time of waiting, the time of waiting is sometimes still long. Through it all, we must remember whatever hurts your heart touches the heart of God. He sees your pain. He hears your cry as Scripture makes known to us the one who joins himself to the Lord is one spirit with Him.[16] We must also remember, "Hope deferred makes the heart sick, but desire fulfilled is a tree of life," as told to us in Proverbs 13:12 (NASB95).

Chosen by God, we have been called to serve a divine purpose. Called to let others know His name. Called to give Him the glory on paths that do not lead down the easy road where the grass is green and the flowers are always in bloom. In moments of feeling extreme discomfort, sometimes we forget that as Christ suffered so will we suffer,[17] and in this world we will have trouble.[18]

Often our walk is tested. When it comes to God's chosen people, our lives are consistently under attack while at the same time we are challenged by the words of Apostle Paul to live a holy life in an unholy and darkened world. We become challenged when we see and learn about people suffering and many suffering needlessly behind a broken world system. Behind the hands of man. Though we may not see immediate results that tame the churning waters, believing prayer invites God to intervene in our present circumstances which builds a foundation not easily shaken.

This brings to mind again many who were called by God, yet they endured extreme conditions as they walked out their destiny. Ruth and Naomi and Job as mentioned already, and Joseph, and as noted previously, Daniel in the lion's den. And Paul in the New Testament who was imprisoned and flogged, beaten and stoned yet his life story opens the eye to see in the whirlwind and the storm is often God's way. There is victory in the end. So whether it is God's sovereign will or His permissive will that allows man's will to rise to the surface, God has the final say.

When it comes to rough patches of life that don't seem to match up with God's promises, not too long ago my friend Marie pointed out that sometimes as it happened with Father Abraham it happens with us too. We arrive in our promised land and figuratively speaking, like Father Abraham we dwell in tents when our present circumstances don't line up with God's promises. Looking through our eyes, our reality looks nothing at all like we

---

16. I Corinthians 6:17 (NASB95).
17. Philippians 1:29, 30. (NASB95).
18. John 16:33.

expected. But in the eyes of God, what we naturally see is temporal because what God speaks and has spoken is already done. Our present conditions are a test of our faith. A test not intended for us to fail but to draw us closer to God as we live out circumstances we cannot explain. In the whirlwind and the storm we find is often God's way in carrying out a divine assignment while at the same time, others' assignments might appear quite different in looks and length of time. Best to keep out eyes centered on God because all assignments from the hand of God prove to have the same marking—God's undeniable presence.

While trying to understand a situation someone close to me was facing, I rose early one morning around 5:00 a.m. petitioning God on their behalf, and I commanded any mountains standing in the way to be removed and cast into the sea. I did not understand the calamitous turn of events I saw my loved one was facing so I sought God in His Word and He led me straight to the Book of Job, Chapter 42, Verse 5. After suffering traumatic events, here we find Job declaring, "But now my eyes see Thee." While reading Job's declaration, I wondered how this could be, and I also questioned what did it have to do with the situation I was seeking God about. I thought about the words in the Bible that declares no one can see God and live[19] so something else must be going on with Job's announcement that he saw God with his eyes. Glancing down at my footnotes, it hit me. Something I had not captured before to explain Job's statement is that God's presence is not seen with our eyes, but with our heart. In explaining the catastrophic events Job suffered, my Bible footnotes affirm, "No form of God appeared in the whirlwind, but what God revealed about Himself enabled Job to see Him."[20] Seeing the God of the Bible as we presently know Him does not involve the eyes, but the heart.

When God chooses you and me, His favor rests upon us. But then we learn His favor often leads to suffering. Suffering by the hand of the enemy. Suffering at the hands of people you hardly know and sometimes from those you do know. In the whirlwind and the storm is God's way. I've come to understand the greater the attack, the greater the call.

Some 40 years ago while sharing with my former Pastor Leroy Gainey a situation I was encountering at work, he looked at me and said, "Vera, you are always going through something." And he was right. Five books later, I acknowledge to you Pastor Gainey, you were right. I've often thought

19. Exodus 33, Verse 20.
20. New American Study Bible (1995).

about his comments and at one point as mentioned in another story, Pastor Gainey looked at me while he shook his head and expressed, "Vera, that's real persecution." I was young in the faith at the time he made this comment. I was struggling to understand what God desired for me to realize about His hand upon my life, but I understand now. Again, it took me years to see it, and five books later to finally understand the words God had spoken to my heart years ago about His favor upon my life. If you haven't realized it yet, with God's favor comes fierce attacks from the enemy of our soul. When we are called by God, we can expect it. So don't let the enemy quiet the life stories God has given you to tell of His mercy and His grace and His involvement in your life story. From my walk with God, He has called me to write inspiring life stories from His heart to my heart so others can know His name.

Much desired by God's chosen people of old, we too look for a new season breaking forth. A season of rest from the bitterness of life unfolding all around us. A season to enter into a place of rest as God has already determined. A place of rest that resonates with where He led His chosen people of old to experience when they walked in seasons of rest for some 20 years and more. We look forward to the day God's promised plan unfolds for this nation and for us individually. What does the Word of God proclaim about our faith to believe? "If you had faith even as small as a mustard seed, you could say to this mountain, 'Move from here to there,' and it would move. Nothing would be impossible."[21] Understanding and applying God's word takes precedence over everything else in life. His declared word reassures our heart about the truth of His character and His enduring promises both for now and for the coming future.

> Amos 4:13. For behold, He who forms mountains and creates the wind and declares to man what are His thoughts, He who makes dawn into darkness and treads on the high places of the earth, the Lord God of hosts is His name. (NASB95)
>
> Galatians 6:9. And let us not lose heart in doing good, for in due time we will reap if we do not grow weary. (NASB95)
>
> Hebrews 11:27. By faith he left Egypt, not fearing the wrath of the king; for he endured, as seeing Him who is unseen. (NASB95)

---

21. Matthew 17:20. (NLT).

Something About Knowing God

Know Who You Are

Earlier in this book, I mentioned the importance of knowing you are whole and complete despite the opinions of others. We can live this truth when we choose to believe who God says we are. When we are secure in who we are in Christ, our sense of acceptance don't come from people. But sometimes we may find that we need help to rid ourselves of old shackling thoughts. What we ultimately believe, what serves as our personal conviction and our anchor is crucial for recognizing and accepting who we are in Christ. Quoting words of wisdom to ground our faith in knowing just who we are proclaim, ". . .godly convictions withstand the changing winds of opinion and the persuasive arguments of opponents. If we're grounded in the Word and we trust what God has said, we can stand firm. Confidence breeds the courage to remain strong amid the conflicts that arise."[22]

I believe the timely and inspired words from my walk with God that are spread across the pages of this book can inspire hope to rise in recognizing who you are in Christ, especially if you have lived with years of regret or live with residue left behind a broken and busted life story. As individuals, we learn by hearing something explained in a different way in order for what we've heard to resonate with our spirit so my hope is that some aspect of a life story of mine has met you where you are. It is my hope that my life experiences have touched a situation where you or someone you love may have had to confront. It is my hope that my transparent life stories have filled hearts with sustaining faith to believe and to achieve despite the journey. It is my hope that my life stories have helped to heal brokenness of heart. I pray the journey I have shared will lead you to stand knowing who you truly are in the eyes of God and will empower you to gain a deeper depth in knowing something more about the God of the Bible.

Love is the foundation of our life story and we need to know or learn to recognize expressions of healthy love. Sometimes the very thing that broke us was misguided choices. Or it was because we allowed others to define who we are. Or just maybe we transferred our values before getting to know the other person's true heart. Or as I had to do, maybe you lived with impoverished circumstances that need to fall off your thinking and your life choices going forward. Whatever circumstance that befell you that tried to break you, allow these words of truth as mentioned before to sink

---

22. In Touch Ministries. "Our Convictions—Our Defense." Inspired by The Teachings of Charles F. Stanley. January 19, 2025.

deep within your soul—When you learn who you are in Christ Jesus, your value is not negotiable. You are enough. God made you for purpose. No need to question your self-worth as you let go of toxic people and negative criticism. God shifts things in our circumstances and in our heart to allow us to see ourselves through His eyes. He sifts through the pain of our past to bring us to a place in life that reminds me of the old adage to pick yourself up, dust yourself off, and go on again. But this old adage, I find doesn't tell the whole story because it leaves out an invaluable word of wisdom— Knowing that you are loved by God and by accepting you are enough must become the guiding foundation for *how* you go on again. This time when you get up to go on again you will now know you are headed in the right direction because you know who you are.

Another short story. While growing up, I thought he had it all. Older than me, quoting the Bible, I thought he had it. Thought she had it too. I believe it was Bishop Dale Bronner who said, "Those who are Christ-like find it hard to discern those we love." How true this has been for me. The way I see it now is love is a double sided coin. It works both ways. How good it is to realize you have innate value and to know who you are in Christ Jesus. How freeing it is to understand we have been made righteous in God's eyes and to accept that we are enough. As you walk through life, remember the world loves its own and you will see this as scales fall from your eyes. Remember this truth when facing strong opposition no matter if it comes from those you deeply care about. A smiling face does not always reflect genuine care for you.

After writing these thoughts, I just so happened to come across more old notes I had jotted down on a blank page in the back of my Bible. Although dated 7/8/98, the words I wrote still echo with truth that were captured from a Joyce Meyer's message that spoke on relationships. Quoting from Joyce: "1) You'll have the same spirit as those you spend most of your time with. 2) Why do you want to keep making yourself miserable by trying to make someone else happy? 3) You must separate/remove yourself from the relationship God has not called you to commit to. If God has not enabled you or given grace for you to be there, get out of it. 4) Be careful when you go around miserable people. Spirits attach themselves."

Applying wisdom is key to learning whether learning from past history recorded in the Bible or from our own life experiences or from someone else's life story. Iron sharpens iron because none of us have it all. My hope is that we will choose to exercise discernment when establishing relationships because the people we choose to spend most of our time with reflects something spiritual and personal about us. What brings relationships together should be because the Holy Spirit is drawing us together. Not the flesh. Not the looks. Not tangible things. As shared before, when people show you who they are the first time believe it. Disengage from unhealthy associations with those who may lean on you but you can't lean on them in times of need. Some people we find we simply need to love from a distance. We find that some people are church folks and not God folks.

Now is a good time to ask the question—What are you believing God to do for you? Is it the fulfillment of a God-given dream to take you from where you are to where you desire to be? Or perhaps you desire to meet your soulmate or to begin a family or maybe as it was with Father Abraham at one point in his life, your life doesn't resemble anything at all like God's promised land so you desire drastic change. Whatever the desire living inside your heart might be, to arrive at the place you are waiting for God to bring you to it will probably take investing in something now that will come together later. God is a promise keeper and though it tarries, we wait for it. If God spoke it to you, then wait for Him to bring it to pass as spoken to us in Habakkuk 2:3. Know that any roadblocks and unexpected trying moments cannot stop what God has already set in motion though you might not see it yet. When it comes to any challenge standing in the way of a dream or a hope, it cannot stop God's plan from coming into fruition. Remember that God has already revealed His love for His covenant people when He declared, "No weapon formed against you shall prosper, and every tongue which rises against you in judgment you shall condemn. This is the heritage of the servants of the Lord, and their righteousness is from Me," says the Lord.[23] When we depend on God, His timing is never too late. Even when He delays a matter.

> Ephesians 3:20, 21. Now to Him who is able to do far more abundantly beyond all that we ask or think, according to the power that works within us, (21) to Him be the glory in the church and in Christ Jesus to all generations forever and ever. Amen. (NASB95)

Added Note: Recently, I quietly questioned God why a particular event unfolding in my life did not happen two or perhaps three years ago, and then God answered without speaking a word. In my heart I understood when it comes to times of solitude we may not have understood, these times deliver

---

23. Isaiah 54:17. (NKJV).

a message about our personal relationship with God just as it did for those who answered His call in biblical times. Looking through a spiritual lens, I find that God's appointed time of solitude in one's life has always been a valued practice. While being protected we are also being guided to learn something more about God's nature we never understood before. This is a place where we are strengthened for the days ahead in order to fulfil the call upon our life. As we walk out our journey, God opens the door to new opportunities to fill our life with something that wasn't there before. A good example is a time when I was on my way to experience a new opportunity God had in store for me that wasn't there before. I made a stop along the way when a door opened for me to encourage someone unexpectedly. Although I'd left home a bit later than planned, I just so happened to meet a homeless stranger and after a brief exchange of words, I prayed for him. Then another thing happened quite unexpectedly. After my prayer, he spoke three words that warmed my heart when he quietly expressed—"I needed this." Am I ever so grateful for God's timing for this stranger and me to meet. God's timing is always perfect though it may seem to us that He has delayed a matter or we think we've started out on a journey later than we think we should have. It is a good time to look again at Habakkuk 2:3 and even Hebrews 10:37. God's words ". . .it will not delay," (Habakkuk 2:3) and His words "For yet in a little while, He who is coming will come and will not delay," (Hebrews 10:37) upon first appearance seems to indicate that events will happen in the moment. But actually, as noted before, it means when God's set timing for these events does occur, they will unfold at that precise moment and not a second later.

Where Do We Go From Here?

So where do we go from here? I pose this question because we are all headed somewhere. Although individually we may need to grow in different areas in our lives, hopefully as believers in Christ we are all headed in the same direction to trust God more fully, to become more determined to look more like His Son in our actions, our attitudes and in words we speak to others as well as our words we voice about ourselves. We are to be mindful about the impact we are making on the world around us, and mindful to uplift and to make known God's great name. Amid the swirling winds of perilous times we see in the world today, I believe we are left with several questions: Does my life actions reveal that I belong to God as turbulent events unfold? Am I striving to stay mindful of God's truth that no weapon formed against me shall prosper? In these times of uncertainty, am I impacting the world around me to make known His great name? Am I striving daily to follow after the leading of the Holy Spirit? It was just the other day I mentioned to my brother that everything we accomplish in God-given assignments or whatever we accomplish in the midst of whatever we are facing is not achieved without first overcoming a challenge. When facing what appears to be insurmountable obstacles, we should ask ourselves, "What would Jesus do?"

If the path we have chosen leads to growth in our personal relationship with God, surely we are headed in the right direction. Weaved throughout this path is a heartfelt desire to make it our business to put God above everything else. When we choose His way not only do we find peace within our soul, our life unfolds according to His perfect plan though oftentimes we wait for the fruit to manifest.

As believers in Christ, we are on a spiritual journey. So how do we remain strong in our dependence upon God when faced with trials that often cause our knees to tremble or our thoughts to race? A few key things come to mind—keep a prayerful attitude and remain consciously aware of God's presence even during the silence. Quiet our inner voice to submissively listen for God's voice of instruction. Remain constant in our reliance on the Bible to find answers to life questions while understanding that God will also speak to a listening heart. Recall God's past triumphs. Mediate on His word to drown out the ridiculing voice of the enemy. Rejoice in His presence which uplifts our countenance. Applying God's word is the glue that holds life together. And remember God is a promise keeper. We need only believe.

Mentioning God's promises brings to mind a story written in one of my previous books that I believe is worth mentioning again. When my oldest grandson was about five years old, when I picked him up after his Sunday school class ended, his teacher reached out her arm to stop me. She shared with me that she had announced to the class there's nothing God cannot do. Then she told me that my grandson raised his small hand and replied, "Yes, there is. God cannot lie." With amazement glistening in her eyes, she looked at me and said, "I have to stay on my toes with Victor!" A couple years later, while reminding my grandson of the words he spoke to his Sunday school teacher, this time he added to what he already said by expressing, "God cannot lie, and he cannot fail." Now how's that for a little one to speak at such a tender age? Truly these are two things God cannot do and aren't we glad about it! We can trust God even after doors have closed. We can trust God even after man has said, "No." It's like the time many years ago when arriving home from work, I saw a foreclosure notice taped to my garage door. In a very short period of time, God not only overturned the words printed on the paper, but the mortgage company offered me a new payment option that was less than half my current monthly mortgage.

So where do we go from here? The right choice is to choose the path that leads to trusting the only true and living God who controls it all. May we choose to respond to the Holy Spirit's gentle leading in the smallest of matters and may we seek to recognize God's presence in our life story. May we choose to honor God's word and persist in prayer and strive to apply His word to every known situation and to situations that unfold unexpectedly. May we not forget the awesome displays of God's majestic power we witness today and His divine splendor witnessed in the past when He parted the Red Sea at just the right moment and defeated enemies too numerous for His people to count. Our God remains the same God of the Bible so may we never forget He has shown Himself to be faithful time and time again. That He heals and He sets things in motion no man can stop. When we can remember during the harshest of times that God asks the question, "Is there anything too difficult for Me?" we can encourage our own faith to believe. When choosing personal relationships, may we choose godly relationships with a nurturing spirit that show mutual care. Everybody is not on the same level, so be mindful of this in your choice of relationships. As my grandson Victor recently wisely expressed, "You can't be friends with somebody who doesn't have a moral compass. Who doesn't share your same value for human life or life on earth period." And finally, avoid leaning too heavily on any one person to the point you feel crushed without them. We all feel pain behind the loss of someone we considered as a friend, but our anchor must be in the Lord our God.

Before completing this book, a small but significant event occurred. One morning around 4:00 a.m., God spoke to my heart the words of Philippians 4:6. Earlier, I had confessed to Him that I didn't know what to do about a pressing matter, and it was at this very moment I heard God speak the words of this Scripture to my heart. After obeying what I saw outlined in this Scripture, immediately I was nudged in my heart to read the next verse. Verse 7 affirmed for me that God had seen the words I had written only moments ago in my journal where I written that all anxiousness had left me. In Verse 7, it notes what takes place in a heart free of anxious thoughts when it declares, "And the peace of God which surpasses all comprehension shall guard your hearts and your minds in Christ Jesus." God was letting me know He knew exactly where I was at the moment I believed His word. But He wasn't done yet. After confessing to God that I had carried out what He instructed me to do, I said, "It is now up to You to do what You said You would do." Again God nudged my heart as He led me to turn to Deuteronomy 26:14. What I saw here is Moses asserting he had listened to the voice of the Lord his God and had done all that God commanded him to do which only moments ago was the very thing I had done. But then Moses spelled out exactly what he wanted God to do which is something I had not done, yet I believe God saw the hope living inside my heart about a certain thing I needed Him to do. Oh, how good it is to know something about knowing God. When we walk in intimate fellowship with Him, He follows us closely. He knows exactly where to lead us in His written Word to take hold of something He wants us to understand when He leads us to Scripture that speaks to our pressing situation. As Scripture declares, "Draw near to God and He will draw near to you" (James 4:8).

Amazingly, two weeks later, God came again to address another cry of my heart concerning someone I care deeply about. This time, instead of speaking to my heart, He led me to read encouraging words in the Bible that spoke to a situation my close friend was battling. What God revealed to me is He saw my friend as whole and redeemed even though I saw questionable moments in my friend's behavior. Something about knowing God which I've come to realize is He doesn't always reveal every event that will take place before His answer to our prayer manifests. For me, this is where believing faith is needed. We believe because God said it, not because of what we see at the moment. An aspect about God's divine nature I've come to also understand is when something troubles our heart, He takes note of our pain as I mentioned already. We arrive at understanding in earth shattering moments more often than not, breakthroughs come on the heels of adversity. Although we may grieve, we must allow ourselves to heal.

I believe we can all agree with this truth when arriving at understanding something about knowing God. Some situations God addresses rather quickly while for others, He addresses over time. I've learned that my understanding of time is not the measure God uses. The path and timing God chooses will always reveal His awesome glory as He sets the captives free who harken to His voice. As also mentioned before, coming to understand something about knowing God extends over a lifetime. It encompasses our past and present journey which includes everything we've learned about God and things we may have forgotten, especially in recalling God's past deeds of deliverance. Learning something about knowing God also encompasses things we have learned from someone else's life story and from their testimonies which help to shape things we all have in common.

One day there will be new heavens and a new earth as foretold in the Bible, and life as we know it will change. If we've chosen a path to live independent of God's sovereign will or chosen to remain comfortable living a lukewarm life, the time to repent is now. But we know without conviction, there is no repentance. Sadly, loving sin can then become more important than loving God.

Something I mentioned in the beginning of this book which is also stated above when getting to know something about knowing God is learning things I did not know before. Recently, while studying the Bible my eyes opened to see the very conditions spoken about in Ezekiel Chapter 13, specifically in Verses 18 and 19 mirror events we see taking place in the world today. The words in these two verses of Scripture speak truth to lives being taken in our own land today while lives are reserved in foreign lands. In the eyes of God, all life is valuable but the fact remains as the Book of Revelation makes clear—there are God's people and there are also those who are sent from the synagogue of Satan. Noted in a few verses that appear before Verses 18 and 19 of Ezekiel Chapter 13, it mentions a flooding rain will come and hailstones will fall; and a violent wind will break out and

Something About Knowing God

God declaring, "And you will know that I am the Lord."[24] Today we have witnessed these same weather patterns. I believe God is speaking to those with ears to hear concerning the times we are living in now. We see Old Testament Scriptures bringing light to life today. Am I ever so thankful that God leads us to words written in the Bible that speak to situations we face today, both personally and nationally.

In summing up the answer to the question of where do we go from here, may we embrace quiet strength and not seek for validation from others who don't even know our purpose. May we accept that we are enough, that we are whole and complete made in the image of God. May we see ourselves as more than our pain if old lingering pain is still there. May we value commitment based on a foundation of faith in our Lord and Savior. May we value loyalty. May we lend our voices and our actions to heal and not harm, and may we choose God because God chooses us. Everything He did, He did for you and me. In everything we accomplish, may we choose to believe and to accept the truth as proclaimed in John, Chapter 15—"Apart from Me, you can do nothing."[25] Any successes achieved, any noteworthy accomplishments attained is not wrought by human strength alone. My hope is that we choose to love with unselfish concern for others[26] and to walk circumspectly in this darkened world. My hope is that we rest in knowing who we are in the eyes of God and that we do not mix our light with the darkness prevalent in this world system, but instead choose to "Have nothing to do with the fruitless deeds of darkness, but rather expose them."[27] May we strive to know what freedom in Christ looks like, smells like and is.

Everything we see taking place in the world today is clearly pointed out in Second Timothy, Chapter Three where we are told that men have become lovers of themselves, family members have turned against family members, children walk in disobedience, the heart of man has waxed cold. There are wars and rumors of wars. Nation rise against nation, and famines and earthquakes and other calamities are all taking place as God forewarned. Although there is nothing new under the sun, these patterns of behaviors are taking place at an all-time high while God's voice continues to call out for people to know His name. For people to be saved from the sentence of eternal separation from God meant only for Satan and his

24. Ezekiel 13:14b. (NASB95)
25. John 15:5.
26. AMP 2015.
27. Ephesians 5:11. (NIV)

fallen angelic host. As Michah 6:8 exhorts, "He has told you, O man, what is good; and what does the Lord require of you but to do justice, to love kindness, and to walk humbly with your God?"[28] Although spoken during Old Testament times, the heart of God has not changed in how He feels about injustice. In His day, Christ constantly challenged injustice and God throughout the Bible addressed issues concerning injustice as well He spoke on injustices we see today while the Book of Revelation reveals the final triumph of justice over injustice. We can learn lessons from biblical times so we won't fall short in our behaviors today. It all comes down to mankind choosing the right path by making the right decision. From words captured long ago that still breathe life today—May we not be found preferring the fulfillment of pleasure to the discipline of our faith.[29] And may we choose to be set apart and not avail ourselves to opportunities that are not from the hand of God.

May we realize as children of God, we play a redemptive role in His plan for mankind because He has predestined us to be conformed to the image of His Son[30] who is our Savior. When we choose God's way we become useful as His hands and feet in reaching the lost, the needy, and the oftentimes forgotten. Something worth keeping close to heart about knowing God is it is never too late for His perfect plan to unfold in a life while life is still lived here on earth. God seeks to mold us as instruments of change to take us outside the walls of the church. As instruments of change, we are to follow in the footsteps of Second Corinthians 6:14 where we are forewarned—we are to have no fellowship with darkness. We are not to walk in darkness, but rather, we are to lend our light to build up the despairing and to bring truth to those perishing. To uphold justice. Our walk before God speaks louder than a title. It speaks louder than religion. It speaks louder than positions in the church when the principles of the church are not found operating in those sitting on the pews or standing at the altar or preaching from the pulpit. May scales fall from our eyes.

As Paul proclaimed in his letter to the Philippians, "Do nothing from selfishness or empty conceit, but with humility of mind let each of you regard one another as more important than himself; do not merely look out for your own personal interests, but also for the interests of others."[31]

---

28. NASB95.
29. Zions Fire. Reverend Dan Hayden. November/December 2000.
30. Romans 8:29, 30.
31. Philippians 2:3. (NASB95).

And I love the way Paul spoke in his letter to the church of Corinth when he ended First Corinthians Chapter Thirteen with these insightful words of wisdom—"But now abide faith, hope, love, these three; but the greatest of these is love."[32] So let us not neglect cherishing those whom God loves. There is a better way than much of what we see taking place in our world today. The better way is Christ Jesus. Now let's get busy.

> Colossians 3:1–4. If then you have been raised up with Christ, keep seeking the things above, where Christ is, seated at the right hand of God. 2. Set your mind on the things above, not on the things that are on earth. 3. For you have died and your life is hidden with Christ in God. 4. When Christ, who is our life, is revealed, then you also will be revealed with Him in glory. (NASB95)

---

32. NASB95.

Revelation 3:20–22

20. Behold, I stand at the door and knock; if anyone hears My voice and opens the door, I will come in to him, and will dine with him, and he with Me.

21. He who overcomes, I will grant to him to sit down with Me on My throne, as I also overcame and sat down with My Father on His throne.

22. He who has an ear, let him hear what the Spirit says to the churches.

(NASB 1995)

Also by Vera L. Smith

Your Creation Declares Your Glory!
When God Spoke To Me, He Said . . .
From My Heart To His Heart
A Hilarious Moment!

Author's Biography

BORN IN A FAMILY of twelve siblings, I grew up in the projects of a small and impoverished section of a Midwest town. From my early childhood and for a number of years that followed, God led me down a path of walking through immense struggles and unexpected heartache in seasons immersed in uncertainty all the while not knowing that one day my struggles would entwine with my life's purpose. I can look back now and recognize everything I experienced in life while clinging to God's hand resulted in gaining wisdom and revelation in the knowledge of God which has helped me to know Him better. This journey has shaped me to write the books I write to encourage others to know Him better through illustrating a personal relationship with the God of the Bible. My journey with God has forged an intense awareness of His nature as revealed through this chosen clay vessel. True to God's nature and word, He opens doors to a future and a hope.

    The real-life narratives written on the pages of my inspired books, I believe, tells of God's glory and His faithfulness and power to transform and to redeem lives from the ashes of a dismal past. This book uncovers the boldness for me to step out of my comfort zone to speak about my mother's untimely and tragic death that took decades before sharing. In writing this book, I recognize another life-changing truth about knowing God. He prepares us for every part of our journey even when we don't realize it. This time while writing, God opened my eyes to understand several key reasons He often led me to walk through seasons of solitude. Not only is God protecting us during these season for reasons we may not have understood before, but times of solitude fulfill the need to hear His voice with clarity and purpose to expand His influence here on earth. It is also a time to deepen our trust in Him.

    Looking beyond any human achievements, it would not be any personal accomplishments that highlight my journey. For me, it is knowing

Author's Biography

God as the author and finisher of my faith and His call upon my life to write and to speak encouraging and liberating words to help others on their journey. From working in the corporate world to the private sector, am I ever so thankful that God used me as His instrument to bring awareness to His name in the midst of challenging moments and in many trying moments others around me were facing. Surely God has a way to carry out His purpose to make others within our reach to become aware they have a decision to make in choosing whether to know Him.

While walking this journey, I was blessed to graduate Summa Cum Laude from undergrad school past the age of 60 which surprised one of my brothers. Years earlier, I graduated with Highest Honors from a local community college. Amongst reaching other endeavors, a few of the greatest honors bestowed on me from the hand of God are the times He used me to speak inspirational messages to Bay Area radio listeners, and more recently, to encourage others through podcast. Some years ago, I shared teaching an adult Sunday school class alongside a young man from Africa who was attending theology school. I am ever so thankful God also gave opportunities for me to participate in motivational speaking events within the church. Through it all, God has faithfully shown me He is my life story. He is my testimony. This fifth book as with my previous books was written while walking alone with God. From cover to cover enjoy captivating real-life stories that provide focus-driven insight to overcome personal life struggles. Become engaged in heartfelt life stories that connect with the presence of God. Then walk away in renewed confidence and the motivation to pursue a deeper trust in the God we know when facing challenges common to us all that can lead to embracing an overcoming spirit! We are called to make a difference outside the walls of the church building.

Author's Biography

God is bigger than any challenge or tragedy we encounter in life. Packed from cover to cover with spiritual, reflective and personal insight that sheds light on overcoming trying moments we share in common, the heart is stirred to glean life-changing messages and to embrace divinely-guided principles from a journey that began with unimaginable heartbreak faced as a young child. Venturing down a path filled with twists and turns during seasons of lack and in times of not knowing where I was headed, to moments of wielding believing faith to walk victoriously has led to writing inspiring real-life stories to renew hope living inside this word of truth—God does not leave His people where they are. A willing heart in the hands of God opens the door to purpose, even later in life. This book can redefine understanding God's presence through a spiritual lens during moments of unrest while it encourages change of thought, if needed, and at times a change in direction to embrace an overcoming spirit. Not only will you be amazed to learn how God showed me that I was healed from a traumatic childhood beginning, but I believe by reading this book you will resonate with this truth—to intimately know God's name is to walk in His nature and to embrace all that makes Him who He is.

From cover to cover, transparent details of a life journey infused with relevant biblical history and Scripture ignites the faith to embrace a deeper understanding to capture divine messages that can be overlooked during moments of unrest or victory or while engulfed in solitude longing to hear God's voice. Walk with me as I share something so deeply personal that

Author's Biography

God never meant for me to carry and neither should you carry what God is ready to heal.

The down to earth real-life experiences on the pages of this book provide opportunities that spur your heart to take hold of small intimate details of knowing something more about God's presence, His divine principles, and His voice as He speaks life messages through a clay vessel with a willing heart to listen. Enjoy the breadth of uplifting and challenging moments that became transformed in the hands of God to add value where value was once hidden. We are on the same journey—to help heal the wounded, to bridge the divide for those who don't know how precious they are in the eyes of God, and to influence others to come to know God's great name and His divine nature. So go ahead and read the book to enjoy an inspiring journey immersed in the presence of God that birthed pearls of wisdom not only to survive in life, but to thrive—from brokenness to wholeness.

Bibliography

Colwell, Robert. In-house sermon, 9/11/24.

Daily Devotion (online). Inspired by The Teachings of Charles F. Stanley. "Confronting Conflict." September 14, 2024. https://sermons-online.org/charles-stanley/devotion/confronting-conflict-202409140005.

Daily Devotion (online). Inspired by The Teachings of Charles F. Stanley. "Victory Over Unforgiveness." November 20, 2024. https://sermons-online.org/charles-stanley/devotion/victory-over-unforgiveness-202411200004.

Furtick, Steven. Online sermon. *Overwhelmed by Life's Demands*. 10/15/2024. https://sermons-online.org/steven-furtick/overwhelmed-by-lifes-demands.

Gibran, Khalil. The Epoch Times (online). 11/16/23.

Hayden, Dan. *Zions Fire*. November/December 2000.

In Touch Ministries. Your daily devotion for 08/07/2024. Inspired by The Teachings of Charles F. Stanley. "Embracing Your Fiery Trials."

In Touch Ministries Daily Devotion (online). Inspired by The Teachings of Charles F. Stanley. "Overcoming Failure." November 19, 2024. https://www.intouchaustralia.org/read/daily-devotions/overcoming-failure.

In Touch Ministries (online article). Inspired by The Teachings of Charles F. Stanley. "The Power of Prayer." November 14, 2024. https://www.intouchaustralia.org/index.php/read/daily-devotions/the-power-of-prayer-2.

In Touch Ministries. "Our Convictions—Our Defense" (online). Inspired by The Teachings of Charles F. Stanley. January 19, 2025. https://www.intouch.org/read/daily-devotions/our-convictions-our-defense.

Keys, James D.. In-house sermon, *Here Today, Gone Tomorrow*. 03/23/2025.

Norful, Smokie. Online sermon. *God is Able. He Did That*. 10/07/2024. https://www.youtube.com/watch?v=1GWR5M3Vjm4.

Steven Darby Ministries. Online sermon. *It's In The Family*. April 22, 2013. https://www.youtube.com/watch?v=W7lZXGQoiE8.

Sweeney, Christopher. Online sermon. September 22, 2024. *Love, the Greatest of All*.

Swindoll, Chuck. Quote. (Nd)

Washington, Denzel. Quote. YouTube online reel. September 29, 2024.

Index

Armor of God, 44–47
Assignment (of God), 5, 39–40, 49, 57, 69, 71, 92

Battle(s), xx–xxi, xxvi, 11, 16, 26, 39, 45, 60, 71–71, 84
Betrayal, xx, 1, 5, 7–8, 38, 63–64, 80
Broken(ness), x, xv, 1, 3–4, 49, 50, 53, 69–70,
Building A New Foundation, 55–59

Faith, x, 10, 12–13, 18, 25, 30–31, 33, 35, 37, 39, 41–44, 46–47, 49–50, 52, 60, 70, 78–81, 84, 92–94, 99, 101–4, 107–9
Fear, Fearful, xix, 3, 11, 30–36, 39–40, 49, 71, 93

God (from cover to cover)
Grace, ix, x, xxiv, 5, 7, 11, 23, 35, 44, 68, 72–74, 84, 93, 95

Heal(ed), Healing, (Healer), ix, x, xii, 5, 13, 21–25, 30, 37, 44, 50, 53, 63–65, 69–70, 78, 94, 99, 101–2, 109–10

Holy Spirit, xxiii, 2, 5, 20–21, 35, 53–54, 59, 64–65, 79, 86, 96, 98, 99

Munroe, Myles, xxi,
Meyer, Joyce, 95

Pray, Prayer(ful), xv–xvi, xix–xx, 2, 4, 6–9, 11, 15–16, 19, 21, 34–35, 42–43, 46, 51, 57, 61, 64, 67, 72, 80, 87, 91, 94, 97–99, 101

Silence, xii, xxiv, 5, 13, 49, 61, 64, 90, 98
Stanley, Charles F., xix, 12–13, 34, 65, 67, 94
Swindoll, Chuck, 15

Territory (Unchartered, Unfamiliar), 10, 31–32, 40, 70, 71, 75

Wait(ing), xiii, xxiii, 5, 7–9, 13, 16, 19, 26, 28, 42, 54, 60, 66, 69–70, 73, 76–77, 81, 91, 96, 98
Whole(ness), ix, x, 1, 5, 24, 38, 85, 94, 100, 102, 110

www.ingramcontent.com/pod-product-compliance
Lightning Source LLC
Chambersburg PA
CBHW070454090426
42735CB00012B/2550